The New Laws of Love

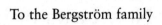

The New Laws of Love

Online Dating and the Privatization of Intimacy

Marie Bergström

polity

Published in association with INED Éditions

First published in French as *Les nouvelles lois de l'amour: Sexualité, couple et rencontres au temps du numérique* © Éditions La Découverte, 2019

This English edition © Marie Bergström 2022

Revised and adapted for the English language edition. This book has been through the normal scholarly process of anonymous peer review, carried out both by Polity and by the French Institute for Demographic Studies (INED). It is based on a book originally published in French in 2019 by Éditions La Découverte. The text was translated by Bernard Cohen and substantially rewritten by the author for the English language edition. The translation was funded by INED and CNRS, GIS GENRE. Quotations from original untranslated French sources have been translated by the author and by Bernard Cohen for this edition.

The right of Marie Bergström to be identified as Author of this Work has been asserted in accordance with the UK Copyright, Designs and Patents Act 1988.

First published in 2022 by Polity Press

Polity Press
65 Bridge Street
Cambridge CB2 1UR, UK

Polity Press
101 Station Landing
Suite 300
Medford, MA 02155, USA

All rights reserved. Except for the quotation of short passages for the purpose of criticism and review, no part of this publication may be reproduced, stored in a retrieval system or transmitted, in any form or by any means, electronic, mechanical, photocopying, recording or otherwise, without the prior permission of the publisher.

ISBN-13: 978-1-5095-4351-9
ISBN-13: 978-1-5095-4352-6 (pb)

A catalogue record for this book is available from the British Library.

Library of Congress Control Number: 2021939855

Typeset in 10.5 on 12 pt Sabon
by Fakenham Prepress Solutions, Fakenham, Norfolk NR21 8NL
Printed and bound in Great Britain by CPI Group (UK) Ltd, Croydon

The publisher has used its best endeavours to ensure that the URLs for external websites referred to in this book are correct and active at the time of going to press. However, the publisher has no responsibility for the websites and can make no guarantee that a site will remain live or that the content is or will remain appropriate.

Every effort has been made to trace all copyright holders, but if any have been overlooked the publisher will be pleased to include any necessary credits in any subsequent reprint or edition.

For further information on Polity, visit our website:
politybooks.com

Contents

Acknowledgments	vi
Figures	viii
Sources	x
Introduction	1
Part I The Privatization of Dating	19
1 The History of Matchmaking	21
2 Dating Technicians	39
3 The Keys to Success	58
4 Time for Sex and Love	80
Part II Unequal before the Laws of Love	97
5 Class at First Sight	99
6 The Age of Singles	121
7 Digital Double Standards	142
Conclusion: Private Matters	165
Notes	176
Bibliography	181

Acknowledgments

A great many people have contributed to this book in different ways.

I would first like to thank all the persons interviewed for this research who shared their experiences of online dating but to whom I cannot refer individually. I am truly grateful to Meetic Group for our cooperation, which allowed me to take an original and international approach to user behavior. Special thanks to Héloïse de Monstiers, Stéphane-Laure Bernelin, and Hélène Point for their trust and encouragements.

A big thank you to John Thompson at Polity, who made this publication possible and provided me with valuable advice, and to Wanda Romanowski, Eva Lelièvre, and Alain Blum at INED Éditions for their incredible support. Thanks also to Michel Bozon, who has played an important role in this research as my advisor, and to Eva Illouz for encouraging me to publish this book and helping me to do so. I was delighted to work with Bernard Cohen, who translated several chapters of this book, and Rébecca Lévy-Guillain, who conducted interviews for this project.

I am indebted to all the people who have commented on various chapters of this book, first of all Étienne Ollion, who helped me improve the text in a decisive way. Thanks also to the anonymous reviewers at Polity and at INED Éditions, as

Acknowledgments

vii

well as to Florence Maillochon, Jan Bergström, and Louise Caron. I received valuable feedback on previous versions of this text by Annabelle Allouch, Milan Bouchet-Valat, Thomas Collas, Joseph Confavreux, Thomas Depecker, Claire-Lise Gaillard, Josué Gimel, Gwenaëlle Mainsant, Elise Marsicano, Camille Masclet, Marie Plessz, Clément Rivière, Mathieu Trachman, and Florian Vörös: I wish to thank all of you. My gratitude goes also to Arnaud Régnier-Loilier and Wilfried Rault, who introduced me to the EPIC survey team.

Finally, I would like to thank the institutions who funded this research: the French Institute for Demographic Studies (INED), the GIS Institut du Genre, the Oxford-Sciences Po Programme (OxPo), and the Observatoire sociologique du changement (OSC) at SciencesPo Paris.

I feel incredibly fortunate with my loving and supportive family. After years of publishing in French, I am delighted to be able to share my research with those to whom I owe so much. This book is dedicated to Ulla, Hans, Jan, Linda, Ebba and Oskar Bergström.

Figures

1.1. Front page of *The Matrimonial News and Special Advertiser* (February 1877)   23

1.2. Newspaper publicity for the "computer dating" agency *Compatibility* (*LIFE*, August 1969)   30

1.3. Interface of the BBS Matchmaker   31

1.4. Interface of the Minitel messaging system ULLA   32

1.5. Interface of Match.com (year 2000)   35

1.6. Interface of Tinder (year 2012)   37

2.1. Homogeneity in dating app interfaces: from left to right, Tinder, Bumble, Hinge, happn, and Facebook Dating   42

2.2. Stereotypical branding between love and sex (Match and EasyFlirt)   49

3.1. Rate of use of online dating platforms in France, the United States, and Germany (%)   60

3.2. Ranking of meeting venues in the United States in 2019 and in Germany in 2020 (%)   62

4.1. Time between initial contact and first sexual intercourse among couples in France (%)   84

6.1. Percentage, by age group, of the women and men in the United States who have used a dating site or app at least once   123

Figures   *ix*

6.2. Pyramid of ages, by gender, declared on four
European dating platforms (%)   124
7.1. Share of female and male users initiating contact
on dating platforms in six countries in 2019 (%)   152

Sources

Surveys

ATP	The American Trends Panel wave 56, Pew Research Center, Washington, DC, 2019 (4,860 respondents). For more information, see Pew Research Center, 2020a, 2020b, 2020c.
Baromètre 2016	Baromètre Santé 2016, Santé publique France, 2016 (15,216 respondents). For more information, see Bajos et al., 2018.
CSF	Contexte de la sexualité en France, INSERM–INED, 2006 (12,364 respondents). For more information, see Bajos and Bozon, 2012.
EPIC	Étude des parcours individuels et conjugaux, INED–INSEE, 2013–2014 (7,825 respondents). For more information, see Rault and Régnier-Loilier, 2019.
Eurostat	Eurostat database, 2002–2019, European Union. For more information, see Eurostat, 2020.
GSS	General Social Survey, NORC–University of Chicago–National Science Foundation, 1972–2018 (64,814 respondents). For more information, see Marsden, 2012.

IALP	Internet & American Life Project Survey, Pew Research Center, Washington, DC, 2013 (2,252 respondents). For more information, see Smith and Duggan, 2013.
Pairfam	The German Family Panel release 12.0, German Research Foundation (DFG), 2019–2020 (7,630 respondents). For more information, see Huinink et al., 2011; Brüderl et al., 2021.
PTS	Pew Tracking Survey, Pew Research Center, Washington, DC, 2015 (2,001 respondents). For more information, see Pew Research Center, 2016.

Big Data

Meetic Group Platforms, Meetic Group Europe, 2019:
  Platforms analyzed: Match, Meetic, Ourtime, DatingDirect, Lexa, LoveScout24 and Neu.
  Metadata on: anonymized user profiles (27,709,707 profiles) and contact behavior (824,989,940 exchanged messages).

Interviews

Interviews with users, 2007–2018:
  biographical interviews with 82 French users of dating sites and applications, conducted by Marie Bergström and Rébecca Lévy-Guillain.
Interviews with entrepreneurs, 2009–2019:
  semi-structured interviews with 19 French, US, and Canadian founders or employees of dating sites and applications, conducted by Marie Bergström.

Introduction

Match, Meetic, OkCupid, Grindr, LoveScout, Tinder, Happn, Bumble... These are just a few of the thousands of dating platforms available online today. The first website to specialize in matchmaking appeared in the United States in the mid-1990s and was soon to be imitated. As the internet expanded internationally, competing sites rolled out at a quick pace across North America and Europe. They were joined some twenty years later by mobile phone applications that immediately became immensely popular, especially among the young. In the past two decades, these platforms have remapped the landscape of dating across much of the western world and beyond, changing the way people meet partners, but also challenging our ideas about sex and love.

The change is remarkable. Since at least the nineteenth century, personal ads, marriage brokers, and other "lonely hearts" networks have offered their services to bring single people together and match prospective partners. Today's dating sites and apps are the direct descendants of those earlier forms of mediated dating; in fact they have inherited many features from their ancestors. What is fundamentally new, however, is their popularity. Until the advent of the internet, the use of commercial matchmaking remained a marginal and marginalized practice. In the 1980s and 1990s, surveys carried out in the United States and in France showed that approximately fewer than 1 in 100 people had met their spouse through a matrimonial ad or agency, for example (Bozon and Heran, 1989; Laumann et al., 1994). In the ranks of the heterosexual population, to resort to such services was taboo; the companies were generally distrusted and users consisted predominantly of divorced and widowed individuals. Mediated dating was considered something of an outcast behavior in the world of dating.

Digital platforms have brought about a major shift. Dating sites and apps have become a common way of meeting partners, and this behavior has lost most of its former social stigma. Users come from all social milieus and background and, unlike older forms of matchmaking, these new ones appeal primarily to young people. The most recent survey carried out in the United States – the birthland of online dating – showed that 30% of American adults had already used a dating site or app in 2019. Among 18- to 29-year-olds, the percentage rose to 48% (Pew Research Center, 2020c). As online dating became commonplace, commercial matchmaking finally emerged from the shade, to reach a broad general public.

What made this change possible? How do we explain this unprecedented success of online dating, and what are the implications? To answer these questions is to draw a portrait of modern love and contemporary sexuality. This is the aim of the present book. By looking at dating and how it changes online, this book tells a new story of the transformation of intimacy, a story that differs considerably from what is currently said about this phenomenon.

Dominant discourses on online dating

The spread of online dating has not gone unnoticed. From the outset, the use of online platforms has commanded considerable attention from the media, essayists, and social scientists. One reason is interest in the phenomenon itself; but an even stronger reason is that online dating is considered to be a mirror of contemporary society. In it we tend to see reflected our hopes, and more often our fears, about the time we live in, about the new sexual norms and the future of social ties. The image that current writings on online dating projects is often an ugly one. It emerges from two main discourses that have largely come to frame popular understandings of online dating.

First, online dating is said to have profoundly changed sexuality by favoring short-term sexual connections at the expense of stable relationships. The term "hookup culture" is often used to describe the new paradigm (Wade, 2017). Although coined initially with reference to American campus culture, today it is used in a broader sense. The term has no exact translation in other languages, yet it resonates strongly with debates on online dating in many European countries. The core idea is that new sexual norms, together with the new technology, have made young people – sometimes referred to as the "Tinder generation" – unwilling to commit or incapable of commitment; they cast aside love and embrace casual sex instead. In particular, online dating would be responsible for the "banalization" of sex, its becoming as mundane as any leisure activity. According to French sociologist Jean-Claude Kaufmann, "a hook-up (*nuit chaude*) can now be scheduled as easily as going to the movies" (Kaufmann, 2010, p. 140). This familiar claim is based on the idea that sex is trivialized on the internet. Sometimes presented as sexual liberation, this development is more often depicted as the decay of love (Sessions Stepp, 2007; Freitas, 2013). Authors argue that romantic long-term relationships have been sapped by endless online opportunities of easy and uncommitted sex.

A second dominant discourse presents digital dating as a commodification of intimate relationships. Apps and sites are viewed as a Trojan horse that brings economic logic into the sphere of intimacy. Because dating platforms are supposedly structured as a market – governed by competition, self-marketing, and choice strategies – the outcome, it is argued, is an unprecedented rationalization of romantic and sexual behavior. This thesis is central to the work of Eva Illouz, whose incisive analysis has been highly influential. In her critical analysis of modernity, Illouz denounces the penetration of the "capitalist cultural grammar" into heterosexual romantic relationships (Illouz, 2012, p. 9). Dating websites, she argues, have played a key role in this historical movement: "Internet dating has introduced to the realm of romantic encounters the principles of mass consumption based on an economy of abundance, endless choice, efficiency, rationalization, selective targeting, and standardization" (Illouz, 2007, p. 90). Illouz also stresses the emergence of new sexual norms, to which she refers as a broader trend of "de-structuration of the romantic will" (p. 197). The internet, in combination with other cultural forces such as the rise of feminism and reliance on psychology, causes a loss of belief in love and a fear of commitment. If online dating indeed operates as a marketplace, then it is a "free market of sexual encounters" (p. 10).

These powerful arguments have commanded a vast audience. The idea that online dating revolves around commodification and intense sexualization is widespread, especially in Europe, and has largely dominated the debate in the social sciences (Salecl, 2010; Dröge and Voirol, 2011; Bauman, 2013; Lardellier, 2015). But, while identifying salient features of online dating – such as the standardized platforms, the often transient nature of online relationships, and the selection mechanisms that work in partner choice – these theses fail to tell the entire story. They pave the way for a harsh criticism of online dating, but fall short of capturing its specificity and explaining its success – explaining how and why people use these platforms. Besides, many empirical elements do not support these arguments.

The first such element is the fact that contemporary societies are still structured by a strong couple norm. Although young people have delayed their first union in a couple, a vast majority of them end up forming romantic relationships (Manning et al., 2014; Bellani et al., 2017; Roseneil et al., 2020). A significant proportion of today's couples meet through online dating (Cacioppo et al., 2013; Rosenfeld et al., 2019; Potârcă, 2020) and, while these platforms stand accused of turning users into consumers incapable of committing to one person and settling down, surveys tend to show that partners who meet online actually commit more quickly than those whose encounter stems from other settings (Rosenfeld et al., 2019). The risk of breakup is not necessarily higher for these relationships; in the United States, for online couples, the risk of separation is the same as, or even lower than, for couples who meet in

Introduction 5

physical settings (Cacioppo et al., 2013; Rosenfeld, 2017). Moreover, the transformations of sexuality cannot easily be reduced to, or explained by, a theory of free markets. Online dating may indeed favor casual relationships, but that's a far cry from being a trivialization and deregulation of sex. These platforms are permeated by powerful social norms, and notably by a gendered double standard that pervades the online world and leads men and women to engage in intimate relationships on very different terms (Bergström, 2012; Pinsky, 2019; Lamont, 2020).

The commodification thesis also poses problems theoretically, as it is either too vague or too extreme. If the argument assumes or implies that our behaviours, attitudes, and beliefs are affected by market economy and by our capitalist society, that is of course true. As social agents, we are inherently formed by the institutions and the means of production of our time. Having said that, we haven't said much. But if commodification means that, with online dating, choosing a partner is essentially the same thing as choosing a yogurt in a supermarket or ordering a sweater from an online catalogue, the assertion is a pleasant trope, but it is wrong, too. The social process of couple formation, or casual dating, is significantly different from consumer behavior; it obeys specific norms and follows patterns of its own. As Viviana Zelizer (2005, p. 29) points out, the true relationship between intimacy and economy cannot be accounted for by theories that reason in terms of "nothing but" – as in partner choice is nothing but a market, or online dating is nothing but consumption. The way intimacy is influenced by the economy, as well as by other social forces, is a more complex process. It is a fine-grained investigation of this process that the present book sets out to write.

Such an aim requires attention to both historical change and continuity. Whenever a new phenomenon is examined, there is a danger of referring to a past that is mostly mythical, in other words of depicting a time when love was blind, pure, and authentic, far removed from our contemporary experiences. Criticisms of online dating often stem from nostalgia for a past that never existed, fueled by fears of technological change, sexual transformations, and the ever-tightening grip of economic forces.

6   The New Laws of Love

In steering a course between the fears of some and the enthusiasm of others, the book sets out to tell another story. It relies on a vast empirical investigation and comes to very different conclusions about what online platforms do to intimacy. The major change lies in a *privatization of dating*. As I will show throughout the book, this feature is fundamental for understanding the popularity of dating platforms, the way people use these sites and apps, and the type of relationships that stem from them. The book shows how dating has become a private matter, and reveals the implications of this shift for both intimate and social life. In doing so, it focuses on the heterosexual population. Rather than offering a general overview, which inevitably does injustice to LGBT experiences, it puts the majority group under the spotlight in order to better understand its specificity.

The privatization of dating

There is something dazzling and almost blinding about online dating. By focusing on the most spectacular features of the phenomenon, such as the mass of registered users, ostentatious self-presentations, and profile swiping, one may fail to detect another, seemingly minor characteristic, which is no less important: the *social insularity* of dating platforms. Online dating is detached from other social activities; it occurs outside an individual's ordinary social circles and possibly without their knowledge.

This is surely the most important difference from earlier ways of meeting potential partners. Historically, heterosexual courtship has always been intimately tied to ordinary social settings, for example the neighborhood, the workplace, the church, the school, community activities, and leisure (Bozon and Heran, 1989; Laumann et al., 1994). This means that meeting venues have very much corresponded to the geography of social life. In the nineteenth century, young people in the countryside often met and courted in the fields; a hundred years later, they tended to meet at school or university. Of course, some settings have always been more propitious for seeking and meeting a spouse than others.

Introduction 7

Today's bars, for instance, are certainly more conducive in this regard than supermarkets. But, with the notable exception of prostitution and swinging, there has never been a place allotted specifically and exclusively to heterosexual courtship. This is all the more the case as, at least from the nineteenth century on, finding love in the course of one's everyday life has been an integral part of the romantic script: the initial encounter is expected to be a matter of fate, not something you seek out actively (Corbin, 1994; Bergström, 2013).

Today's platforms, explicitly and wholly dedicated to dating, mark a radical break from this historical pattern. Meeting partners is now a specific social practice, with its own platforms, clearly delineated in space and time, and with an explicit purpose. The real novelty lies here, in the disembedding of dating from other social spheres and in its resulting privatization.

Disembedded matchmaking

To feed and to clothe ourselves, to clean our homes, to nurse our kids and take care of our elderly parents... Over the past decades, we have become accustomed to resorting to private companies for the most intimate activities. When it comes to meeting partners, however, the idea of commercial intermediation was met with aversion for a long time. The dissemination of dating platforms from the 1990s onward corresponds to a progressive "disembedding" of dating. I borrow the term from Karl Polanyi (1944): it refers to a process whereby a series of activities that have previously been embedded in ordinary social relations become detached from society and form an autonomous market sphere.

This extension of capitalism, through the transformation of objects and activities into new products and services, has accelerated remarkably with the new technology. Critics of commodification are correct to point out the growing interconnections between the economy and intimacy. The diversification of technology and the intensification of its uses, which have penetrated so many areas of daily life, have opened up new areas for investment, and private companies are more present than ever in our private lives.

8   The New Laws of Love

Tech entrepreneurs now serve as intermediaries for our social interactions, including the most private ones, for instance communicating with friends and family, sharing photos, coordinating shopping lists and wedding lists, and getting to know people, make new friends, and meet partners and lovers. At the same time, the symbolic boundaries between what is "marketable" and what is "non-marketable" are constantly shifting and spur controversy. As the sociologist Viviana Zelizer observed, economic activity and intimate relations are often thought of as "separate spheres and hostile worlds" with radically different logics, involving rationality on the one hand and emotion on the other, "with inevitable contamination and disorder resulting when the two spheres come into contact with each other" (Zelizer, 2005, pp. 20–21). The expansion of the market into the private sphere has aroused strong fears and is accused of corrupting and "inexorably erod[ing] intimate social ties" (p. 25). The reactions to online dating provide a striking example of these tensions caused by the incursion of private actors into the sphere of intimacy.

Before jumping to the conclusion that intimate relations have somehow been taken over by commodification and rationalization, a key distinction must be made between online dating as an industry – which involves private companies trying to sell their services – and online dating as a practice – that is, how the platforms are used. The market mechanisms ruling the industry do not necessarily and automatically carry over into user practices. Conflating the two would on the one hand lead to a mechanical and deterministic reading of social behavior and, on the other hand, fail to recognize the autonomy of the market. To avoid these pitfalls, I have devoted a specific analysis to the economy of online dating. Despite growing concerns over the role of capitalist market forces in our private lives, there has been surprisingly little academic interest in the companies that operate in the sphere of privacy. This is the case with online dating, where the "market" metaphor, used to describe romantic and sexual interactions, has drawn attention away from the actual marketplace – the actors who create these products, their work, and the norms governing their business (Wilken et al., 2019; Pidoux et al., 2021). The first aim of

Introduction 9

the book is therefore to pry open the black box of the online dating industry.

The main goal is, nonetheless, to investigate the consequences for users. The disembedding of dating means bypassing ordinary social relations in the search for a partner. With digital platforms, dating becomes a private matter.

The transformation of social life

From its earliest days, the internet has raised questions about social ties. Theories and inquiries have differed over time, going often from enthusiasm to severe criticism, as we can see in the work of internet specialist Sherry Turkle. Known to many for her pioneering work on digital communities and identities, Turkle described the internet, in her first books, as a horizontal and fundamentally democratic universe, reflecting an era when computer users were a socially homogeneous and tech-savvy group and when the enthusiasm about networking was huge (Turkle, 1995). Her last books strike a very different tone. In *Alone Together*, the internet is no longer liberating but alienating. Turkle raises the alarm on how social media negatively affect our possibility to create real, authentic, and meaningful relationships, especially among young adults, leaving us constantly connected but more alone than ever (Turkle, 2011).

The idea that social relations are breaking down under the impact of new technology is not new (Hampton and Wellman, 2018). At the very start of the century, Robert D. Putnam outlined this process in his best-selling book *Bowling Alone*, in which he predicted the decline of community in the United States under the influence of new media and technologies, among other factors (Putnam, 2000). Surveys, however, tend to show that exactly the opposite has occurred. A survey by the Pew Research Institute in 2011 showed that individuals who were the most connected were also the ones with the largest and most diverse networks; they had more and closer friends than individuals with less internet activity, and they declared more often to have social support. These results are consistent with those of other studies, carried out in both North America and Europe (Wang and Wellman, 2010; Mercklé, 2011). In France, for instance, social life (e.g. social visits, entertainment, and meals with friends and family) tends to have increased over time (Dumontier and Pan Ké Shon, 1999), and the most digitally connected people have been found to interact more with people in the physical world, and more often (Mercklé, 2011). These empirical observations will surely disappoint the prophets of social disintegration: social life is not in decline but is undergoing a transformation.

I believe the major change to be a privatization of social life. By this term I refer on the one hand to a shift from outdoor to indoor activities, as many practices that previously occurred in public space have migrated to the domestic sphere, and on the other hand to a tightening of social networks, which have become more centered around close intimate relationships. This means that mingling with strangers in public settings has become rarer, while domestic and private socializing has expanded. This evolution is palpable among adults, who spend less time with neighbors and more time with close kin and friends at home, for example (Wellman, 1999), but also in youth culture, where the advent of computers and digital leisure has contributed to a switch from "street culture" to a genuine "bedroom culture" (Bovill and Livingstone, 2001; Livingstone, 2002).

Online dating takes this privatization into the realms of love and sex and accentuates it. This may come as a surprise to observers, who surmise, from the large numbers of users and their public profiles, that these platforms are a new form of public space. Online dating, however, is radically different from meeting at a club, in a bar, or in any other type of public venue. First, the platforms are accessible from home, and hence they turn meeting a partner into a domestic activity. Second, far from having a public setting, interactions are strictly dyadic, being based on one-to-one conversations that cannot be seen or overheard by a third party. Third and most importantly, online dating operates a clear separation between social networks and sexual networks. Whereas previously people met partners in ordinary social settings and often through people they knew, online dating involves circumventing one's social circles.

As Michael Rosenfeld and his colleagues have stressed, this means "disintermediating your friends" in dating (Rosenfeld et al., 2019). But the historical movement at work here is

Introduction 11

much broader. More than just circumventing family and friends, these platforms operate a sharp distinction between dating and *all forms* of sociability, turning the former into a specific social activity, with its own space and time. This is not a mere displacement of other meeting venues, it is a radical shift in the way we approach intimate relationships and organize social life.

This shift from public to private dating was first observed in the LGBT community. Gay and lesbian populations in the western world have seen a decline in community spaces, which earlier were important meeting venues, in favor of online encounters. In Europe the trend is particularly clear among gay men, for whom "the emergence of the internet coincides with lower attendance in spaces that combine sociability and meeting partners" (Velter, 2007, p. 82). This online migration has been harshly criticized by scholars such as Timothy James Dean, who sees it as a "troubling privatization" in which real-life face-to-face encounters have been replaced by solitary sex in front of a computer (Dean, 2009, p. 177). Others, such as Kane Race, have criticized this nostalgic viewpoint, stressing that gay hookup apps are "a significant source of pleasure, connection, eroticism and intimacy" (Race, 2015, p. 256). In any case, online dating participates in a general trend of individualization of homosexual experiences. As many scholars have pointed out, the greater acceptance of homosexuality has weakened the ties of community experience and has made some, often young lesbians and gays, distance themselves from what is sometimes called "the gay scene" (Adam, 1999; Rivière et al., 2015). Sex has become more private, as people meet more often outside collective community structures.

A similar transformation is now underway in the heterosexual population. With the expansion of online dating, the search for romantic and sexual partners is no longer within the bounds of ordinary life. The social surrounding is stripped not only of its matchmaking function but also of control over nascent relationships. This privatization of dating has two major implications: it plays a crucial, though often overlooked role in the success of online dating; and it creates an environment where external control is loosened. The present book will take a close look at these changes; in consequence it

12   The New Laws of Love

will tell a different story of how dating platforms have grown so big and what they are doing to intimacy.

Dating under the microscope

There is today an important body of scientific literature on online dating, although it seldom reaches the audience it deserves, as research is often published in academic journals that remain rather confidential. With some notable exceptions (Schmitz, 2016; Vaughan Curington et al., 2021), most books on the topic are written by journalists and essayists who draw very little on empirical observation. These books often start with an already given story: a hard-cut vision of online dating and its social impact. Although there can be references to scientific findings, and even some fieldwork, the empirical analysis is not as thorough as the theoretical framework may be. Proof is read into theory, and there is consequently very little room for contradicting facts, or even for scientific discovery and surprise. My starting point is different, as I draw on extensive empirical research. This leads me to other conclusions about the nature and novelty of online dating.

Empirical sources and methods
This book is based on research conducted between 2007 and 2020. The project started when dating websites were still a fairly new phenomenon; then it followed the emergence and diffusion of mobile apps later on. The depth of this historical layering helped me avoid overinterpretation and presentism. The empirical material comes mainly from three different sources, which articulate both a quantitative and a qualitative approach. Swedish historian Brita Planck, whose research theme is marriage in the Swedish aristocracy in the eighteenth and nineteenth centuries, gives a good illustration of the importance of such mixed methods. If she were to use only statistical data, Plancks says, she would be tempted to say that marriage is no more than a matter of money and social status, as couples were strictly matched on these criteria at the time. However, if she were to rely solely on qualitative material such as the large body of letters analyzed in her research, she would conclude that, even 200 years

Introduction 13

ago, marriage was all about love and desire. By combining both types of source, she can show that love, as a feeling, is homogamous and strongly linked to class (Planck, 2014, 2018). Studying online dating requires more than ever a dual approach of this sort, as user narratives are full of feelings of excitement, distrust, enthusiasm, frustration, and deception and convey an image of online dating that is sometimes contradicted by statistical analysis, which reveals trends that users do not see (or do not want to see). For these reasons, I attempt to use systematically both qualitative and quantitative sources.

First, I use several large-scale scientific surveys in order to measure and characterize the use of online dating. Surveys on the topic are scarce and prompt me to focus on three countries where data are available and fairly recent: the United States, Germany, and France. The data come from questionnaire surveys, with representative population samples, on couple formation, sexual health, or digital technology (see Sources, pp. x–xi). Analyzing this type of macro data is essential for establishing usage rate, the characteristics of users, and the type of relationships formed online.

Alongside these traditional surveys, I also gathered "big data" from several online dating platforms. This was made possible by a scientific collaboration with the company Meetic Group, owner of several dating services such as DatingDirect, OurTime, French Meetic, Dutch Lexa, German LoveScout24 and Neu. Meetic Group is also the owner of the European activities of Match, which has a large user base in many countries. Access to anonymized and censured data from these seven international platforms permitted me to observe global trends in self-presentation and contact behavior. My analysis was carried out in strict observance of user privacy. This means that I was never able to identify users, track their usage, or access any of their communications. Only metadata were analyzed, as I did not have access to actual profiles or messages. But these data are precious for understanding how users of different backgrounds (age, gender, education, country, region, etc.) use the platforms and what groups interact with whom.

A qualitative study complements this quantitative approach and is based on interviews with 82 French users

14 The New Laws of Love

of dating sites and applications, aged between 18 and 68 years and coming from diverse social backgrounds. Almost all respondents identified as heterosexual; two identified as bisexual. I conducted the majority of the interviews myself; some were conducted by sociologist Rébecca Lévy-Guillain, who participated in the last stage of this project. All interviews were recorded, transcribed, and subjected to an in-depth analysis. The interviews had a biographical character in order to permit me to follow the trajectories of the interviewees. Thus I was able not only to situate the moments at which my respondents used online dating, but also to compare their online experiences with those that took place "offline," in person. The following chapters present many excerpts from these interviews. Names and certain information have been changed in order to protect the anonymity of the interviewees. Readers should be warned that all my respondents lived in France, and experience can of course differ in other countries.

In addition to these interviews with users, I also conducted a series of interviews with founders of dating sites and apps, mainly French but also North American. These interviews aimed to help me understand how founders conceive of their own dating platforms and what visions of the industry they entertain. Because many of them were careful to protect the image of their company and I didn't want them to censure their speech for fear of bad press, their names have been changed and the names of their platforms are not revealed.

Book outline

The book is divided into seven chapters, each focusing on a specific topic related to online dating and the transformation of heterosexual relationships. The first part of the book looks at the process of privatization, which is approached from different vantage points: a historical perspective, an analysis of the dating economy, an explanation of the success of online dating, and an analysis of the changes that this form of dating brings about in terms of sex and love.

Chapter 1 opens up the archives, looking for the origins of online dating. Matching services have a long history in both

Europe and the United States. The first matrimonial agencies and personal ads appeared in the nineteenth century, and forms of "computer dating" were experienced in the 1950s; the first network of matchmaking systems followed a few decades later. This genealogy establishes a strong filiation between earlier services and today's digital platforms. It also reveals a common criticism that targeted them from the start: as early as in the nineteenth century, matchmaking services were accused of corrupting intimate relationships by introducing economic standards. The commodification of intimacy appears as a long-running fear of commercial inter-mediaries rather than as a feature of late capitalism.

Chapter 2 pursues this historical analysis by looking at the emergence of today's online dating market. Drawing on inter-views with the founders of a series of dating sites and apps, it shows the social and professional norms that inform these platforms and govern their creation. Whereas the features of dating platforms are commonly scrutinized for what they supposedly says about modern love, this chapter shows that the products primarily reflect economic concerns. The making of dating platforms obeys contemporary market phenomena, namely isomorphism, segmentation, and stereotyping.

Unlike older forms of mediated dating that never made it into the mainstream, online dating has become a common practice and an important meeting venue in the western world. However, the phenomenon has also been exaggerated, both in the press and by scientific scholars. Using national surveys from different countries, chapter 3 gives an overview of the number of users and the proportion of couples that meet online. It also provides a new explanation for the popularity of online dating – namely that online dating owes its success to the separation it operates between the sexual and the social sphere. This feature is fundamental to *why* and *how* people use online dating, although the reasons differ between young adults, people in their thirties, and separated individuals in mid-life.

Online dating is primarily casual dating. This common perception, largely conveyed by the media, is also a scien-tific fact. Chapter 4 shows that relationships initiated online rapidly become sexual and are often short-term; but it also challenges the common interpretations of this trend. Where

16   The New Laws of Love

authors often see a radical shift in norms, this book insists on a change in *context*. The sexual nature of online dating must, once again, be understood in the light of privatization; individuals more easily engage with and disengage from partners with whom they do not share a social setting. What is more, online dating does not hinder couple formation, nor does it imply some commitment phobia. In fact, the couple norm is as strong as ever, but the ways of committing are changing.

The second part of book looks at the inequalities in dating; we are not all equal before the laws of love. Online dating has not changed this, but it lays bare the discriminations, prejudices, and injustices that characterize the intimate sphere.

Chapter 5 investigates the mechanisms of assortative matching in online dating. The hyper-standardized platforms do not obstruct social differences in user behavior, nor do they prevent online relations from being homogamous. Users tend to interact with people from a social milieu similar to their own. This social selection is not due only to algorithms or predefined preference; it is rather the result of class dispositions and cultural prerequisites. Precisely because online dating takes away some of the most formal obstacles to social diversity, it reveals the strength and the modus operandi of today's social hierarchies.

Although specifically designed to match people as partners, dating platforms have their winners and losers. Not everyone manages to initiate contacts, meet partners, or form a relationship. These inequalities are not only individual but follow strong regularities of gender and age. Chapter 6 shows that young men are often rejected by their female peers who seek contact with more mature men. At older ages, this sexual disqualification turns against female users who, after a separation, show interest in men of their own age, who then turn to younger women. Dating platforms reveal this machinery of matching and those excluded from the process.

The #MeToo movement gave a striking illustration both of the gender inequalities that characterize sexuality and of a change in attitudes that makes these inequalities less and less acceptable. Online dating bears witness to this complex nature of contemporary sexual norms. Dating services are a site for sexual exploration both for women and for men, but internet interactions are also profoundly gendered. This is clear from surveys, big data, and interviews that disclose a dual norm of *male initiative* and *female sexual reserve*. The last chapter looks at these traditional gender roles, which are reproduced online. It highlights the persistent double standard in sexual behavior and the different ways in which women and men are authorized to express desire. Although explicit consent is on the political agenda, the observation of actual dating behaviour shows that it is rarely expressed as such. On the contrary, sexual ambiguity remains the norm in heterosexual relations. The grey areas between consent and abuse are widening, especially online, where sexual desire is acted out but rarely pronounced.

The conclusion develops the main thesis of this book and puts it in a historical perspective. Online dating is both a cause and a consequence of a larger privatization of social life. As public socializing has decreased and, with it, also the opportunities for meeting new people, dating platforms attract users who wish to find partners outside their immediate surrounding. However, rather than installing a new public meeting venue – like the balls of the early twentieth century – online dating makes meeting partners more private than ever, turning it into a solitary and deeply personal matter.

Part I
The Privatization of Dating

1

The History of Matchmaking

There are thousands of marriageable men and women of all ages capable of making each other happy, who never have a chance of meeting... Therefore, the desirability of having some organ through which ladies and gentlemen aspiring to marriage can be honorably brought into communication is too obvious to need a demonstration.

The Matrimonial News and Special Advertiser,
October 1877

Our mission is to create new connections and bring the world closer together and help people meet others they otherwise wouldn't have met.

Tinder, February 2017

Today's dating sites and apps were born with the internet, but they can trace their distant origins to personal advertisements and forms of marriage brokerage that developed in the nineteenth century on both sides of the Atlantic. These early forms of commercial matchmaking have survived until today, but were supplemented in the 1980s by digital dating services such as the bulletin board systems (BBSs) in North America and the Minitel in France. Each of these services is a child of its time. They bear the mark of the sexual norms and matrimonial system they operated in, but also those of the economic and technical environment of their time. The spread is often tied to technological innovations, beginning with industrial printing, which made classified advertising popular, then moving on to early digital technologies, which spurred "computer dating" and the first online dating networks, and finally to the World Wide Web and mobile technology, with the websites and apps familiar to us today.

Many similarities can be found between these different types of dating services. The companies that operated in earlier forms of matchmaking were often the first to invest in new markets, hence features from older services have been passed on and adapted to new platforms. The filiation is noticeable not only in the *production* but also in the *reception* of dating services, as arguments directed against them can be found from time to time. The contemporary view that online dating has commodified intimate relations echoes a nineteenth-century outcry against matrimonial agencies and personal ads for turning marriage into a market. On the basis of work carried out by European and American historians and through an analysis of press archives, this chapter traces the origins of online dating. It shows that many features of these platforms and many debates around them, all considered radically new, are curiously similar to those features and debates found in their ancestors, sometimes 150 years old.

Marriage brokerage and personal ads

One of the first attested marriage advertisements was published in 1692 in the *Athenian Mercury*, an early British periodical (Cocks, 2015). Such advertisements were to remain rare until the second half of the nineteenth century, when "spouse wanted" ads became a staple of some newspapers in the English-speaking world, particularly the popular dailies of London and New York. Cheaper newspapers of mass circulation flourished as a result of the industrialization of publishing and population growth in urban centers. The dailies – typically, tabloids known as "the penny press" – were financed largely through advertising, which included classifieds. The personal columns soon began running matrimonial ads. The *New York Herald*, the largest daily newspaper in the United States at the time, published its first marriage ads in 1855 and was followed by the *New York Times* in 1860 (Epstein, 2010).

Similar advertisements flourished at the same time in London but, as historian Harry G. Cooks points out, "respectable papers like the *Times* or *Morning Chronicle* refused to carry matrimonial ads, thereby encouraging the development of a specialist press devoted solely to publishing them" (Cocks, 2015, p. 22). In Great Britain as in France, these "matrimonial papers" were closely linked to marriage brokerage, which spread around Europe in the nineteenth century (see Figure 1.1). Primarily the matrimonial agencies offered their services to a bourgeois clientele, taking commission on the dowry in cases of successful matches, but the papers (*feuilles d'annonces* in French) allowed them to reach a broader and more socially diverse public (Gaillard, 2017).

Figure 1.1. Front page of *The Matrimonial News and Special Advertiser* (February, 1877)

While the development of newspaper publishing provided the material possibility to circulate classified advertisements, the impetus for mediatized matchmaking came from the social transformations of the nineteenth century. Industrialization and urbanization saw young people move away from their original environment and sever their ties to family- and neighborhood-based social networks, where they would traditionally find a spouse (Cocks, 2013, 2015). Matchmaking services allowed access to new potential partners, especially for those without the right social connections (Gaillard, 2020). However, the personal ads were also very much a product of the nineteenth century matrimonial system. In her doctoral research on French marriage brokerage and personal ads, Claire-Lise Gaillard stresses that, at the end of the nineteenth century, social status, possessions, properties, and dowry were more commonly mentioned in advertisements than the search for love and affection. Marriage was not simply a personal matter but a family concern. It is worth noticing that, at that time, almost a third of the ads published in France were written by parents on the lookout for a spouse for their daughters. Finding a suitable "match" was of utter importance, and the desired social attributes were therefore clearly articulated (Gaillard, 2020).

Contemporaries did not see the emergence of this new business in a favourable light. While ads and agencies were shaped by traditional matrimonial norms, they also clashed with codes of romantic love that had grown strong during the century – for instance that of "companionate marriage," the ideal that "marriage should be based on the true love and mutual affection of marital partners rather than on family ties and parental negotiations" (Phegley, 2013, p. 130). The new matchmaking services came under attack on both sides of the Atlantic as newspapers, novels, and plays either mocked their vulgarity or condemned their negative impact, in terms not unlike those directed today against dating sites and apps. In fact the two most lively debates of the nineteenth century are strikingly similar to how online dating is framed today.

The appearance of matrimonial advertisements and agencies was first caught in a nineteenth-century debate about falling marriage rates. Contemporary observers raised concerns about the growing number of unmarried persons,

The History of Matchmaking 25

which affected how the new matchmaking services were perceived. A common understanding was that in modern society young men and women were having increasing difficulty in finding a spouse, and therefore turned to professional intermediaries. The publishers of matrimonial ads often drew on this idea: when addressing their readers, they evoked the growing prevalence of singles and promoted their services as a solution to the problem.

> Among the serious causes of the shortage of marriages, we do not hesitate to point out the difficulties and embarrassment experienced by most people, of either sex, who wish to marry – not only to seek, but also to find, meet, and get to know their one and only. [...] In this frenzied century – with so many varied pleasures, constant labors, and important business of multiple sorts that must be dealt with at the same time, at full steam – many men whose position requires that they marry promptly enjoy neither the time nor the circumstances to seek and find a wife. (*La Gazette du Mariage*, July 15, 1882)

The publishers of matrimonial ads often stressed the difficulties of meeting someone in a "frenzied" society characterized by the intensification of economic and social life and by a perceived acceleration of time. Young people were thought to be too busy or simply inapt to find a spouse, and marriage was consequently considered to be in crisis (Epstein, 2010; Cocks, 2013). Interestingly, this was actually not the case at all. At the end of the nineteenth century marriage rates were not falling in Europe but were rather stable over time, or even increasing (Hajnal, 1953). What was taken for a fact was in reality a false assumption, spurred by fears that marriage could be in decline (Cocks, 2013).

Today we witness a similar phenomenon. When explaining the popularity of online dating, journalists, bloggers, and essayists almost systematically refer to the rising rates of singlehood. People are perceived as having difficulties, not only with encountering potential partners, but also with committing to stable relationships. Ironically, from this point of view, our hyperconnected world, in which communication is undoubtedly faster and more effortless than ever before, has made interaction and relationship building more complicated

26   The New Laws of Love

than they were in the past. But, once again, empirical data tend to invalidate this pervasive idea. It is true that more people are single in the 2020s than in the 1970s, but this is not due to a hypothetical difficulty in forming couples. Relationship rates are not falling: just as many people form couples today as they did a few decades ago (Manning et al., 2014; Bouchet-Valat, 2015), the difference is rather that they break up more often than before (see chapter 6). That is, it is just as difficult today as it was yesterday to find empirically the supposed crisis of couple formation. What is easy to find, however, is the seemingly timeless fear that marriage and love are under threat and about to disappear. This fear often makes matchmaking services into scapegoats. This is the fate of Tinder today, just as it was the fate of *Matrimonial News* more than a hundred years ago.

The old commodification debate

A second debate with a long history is the one on the commercialization of love and marriage. In the nineteenth century, publishers of personal ads and matrimonial agencies were accused of turning marriage into a money-making business. Popular outcry in the United States demanded a ban on matrimonial advertisements (Epstein, 2010), while jurists in France challenged both the legality and the morality of marriage brokerage, and public opinion was alarmed by the stream of criminal cases involving marriage agencies (Gaillard, 2017). At the same time, indignant articles published both in Europe and in North America accused "spouse wanted" ads of debasing the sacred institution of marriage by reducing it to a commercial exchange. The men and women who used ads and agencies were scorned for taking a pragmatic approach to matrimony. To lay out one's expectations and to proclaim one's own social status in public had all the hallmarks of a commercial transaction. Observers were deeply disturbed by this direct approach to the business of marriage, as it stained the ideal of romantic love (Kalifa, 2011; Cocks, 2013).

During this debate, French nineteenth-century commentators coined the term "marriage market" (Gaillard, 2020). Since then, this term has acquired a scientific character, being

The History of Matchmaking 27

used primarily by scholars in economics to describe partner choice and matching. But when it was coined in France, it was not a concept at all; it was a moral term used to condemn marriage brokerage:

> [The critical essays] readily describe these agencies as an "industry," or even as "marriage factories," in order to awaken the anxieties of a society in full industrialization. In short, the marriage market is supposed to be the expression of a generalized competition between marriageable individuals in a modern society characterized by urban anonymity. The metaphorical use of the term "matrimonial market" aims to morally contest these agencies, as it maintains a confusion between the rationale that governs partner choice and the commercial logic that governs these new businesses. Since the agencies constitute a "marriage market," responding as they do to the demand of their clientele, does this not mean that the couple formations themselves are dictated by the rules of market competition? From observing a matrimonial market to asserting a commodification of people is only a short step. (Gaillard, 2020, p. 50)

This historical perspective brings many insights to the contemporary debate about the commodification of love. Just as their ancestors, dating sites and apps are said to turn intimate relationships into a market, and users stand accused of having a pragmatic, or even consumerist approach to partner choice. In much the same way as industrialization was held responsible a century ago, objections now focus on the liberal market economy. But the arguments are ultimately the same now as they were then, and are found both in Europe and in North America. Pamela Epstein's analysis of how matrimonial ads were covered by the American press in the late nineteenth century reveals that "critics of personal ads saw them as symptomatic of a new era of commercialization and commodification, and feared that the results would be dangerous – not only to individuals but to society as a whole. As the ads multiplied, they provided additional proof that the market was intruding into private life in an unprecedented manner" (Epstein, 2010, pp. 106–107). This diagnosis is very similar to the ones we find around online dating today. While the twenty-first century is often described as a critical moment in history in which capitalism changes and corrupts intimate relationships, a very similar criticism was already mounted against the market some 150 years ago.

The nineteenth century's disapproval of a presumed "marriage market" may seem strange. Why would talk of money, real estate, and heritage when arranging marriage alarm the general public so much at a time when marriage was indeed closely intertwined with economic issues? What shocked this public, Claire-Lise Gaillard explains, was that the economic concerns were so bluntly put on display. Making a good match was important at the time, but these matrimonial negotiations were supposed to remain hidden behind the scenes. The reason why marriage seekers dared to make them public was precisely that the ads and agencies allowed them to remain anonymous. In other words, what appalled the public was not the socioeconomic foundation of marriage in itself, but rather the *exhibition* of this foundation. As Claire-Lise Gaillard puts it, "the market criticism reveals the malaise of the nineteenth-century society to see the real principles of partner choice being exposed in crude terms in the advertising columns, while they usually were kept secret" (Gaillard, 2020, p. 61).

Nineteenth-century observers knew, just as we do today, that love is not blind. People have partner preferences but are reluctant to verbalize them. In an ordinary social setting, these preferences can remain implicit: we approach people in whom we are interested (and ignore others), and so we carry out a non-verbalized selection. But match-making services – whether in print or online – make these preferences explicit and put them on the public scene. To a present-day observer, it is relatively easy to see what the nineteenth-century commentators did not want to admit: that the matrimonial ads and agencies did not themselves *generate* the economic considerations that floated around marriage but made them explicit. In the same way, dating platforms have not created the social, racial, and sexual preferences that play out online – something they are often accused of. They do, however, make these criteria very visible. Thus we can say that dating services *make explicit the terms of partner selection* and, in doing so, challenge our representations of love.

The moral stigma surrounding matchmaking services would lastingly hold them in disrepute, and matrimonial agencies and ads never gained much traction. Even in their heyday, between the two world wars, when agencies were opening with branch offices and greater use of classifieds in major dailies, they remained marginal, according to surveys conducted during the twentieth century. In France in the mid-1980s, less than one couple in a hundred had met through matrimonial agencies or ads, and an overwhelming majority of the French population said that they would never consider using them (Bozon and Heran, 1989). The tone of disapproval echoed the complaints heard one century earlier: the system continued to carry a stigma of commercialization and fraud and was not considered "serious." A survey conducted in the United States in 1992 gives a very similar picture: only 1% of the American respondents had met their partner through a personal ad (Laumann et al., 1994). New digital technologies would nevertheless renew the matchmaking business.

BBS and Minitel networks: praise and prejudice

The first experiments with "computer dating" (Figure 1.2) date back to the late 1950s, when students at Harvard and Stanford used punch cards to match candidates for dates (Gillmor, 2007; Sprecher et al., 2008). A similar arrangement was adopted for scientific purposes in the 1960s, when social psychologists were investigating the factors at work in interpersonal attraction, one of the discipline's pet topics at the time (Coombs and Kenkel, 1966; Byrne et al., 1970). Researchers programmed the computers to match men and women according to a predetermined formula, established on the basis of data from questionnaires, physical attractiveness scales, and personality tests. Dates were arranged and subsequently evaluated after participants submitted their satisfaction questionnaires. The system was also marketed by marriage agencies; one of the earliest to specialize in computer matchmaking was the Scientific Marriage Foundation, which had started business in 1957 (Joyce and Baker, 2008).

Figure 1.2. Newspaper publicity for the "computer dating" agency *Compatibility* (*LIFE*, August 1969)

The agencies introduced men and women who were found compatible in terms of preferences and personality traits, and also homogamous about age, ethnicity, social and occupational status, and religion (Sindberg et al., 1972). Some thirty years later, such experiments were carried over into the automatic matching arrangements available on different forms of computer networks.

When new technologies were introduced in the 1980s, the matching services made great strides. Computers in the United States were networking since the late 1960s, but it was only with the expansion of microcomputing in the 1980s and the introduction of BBSs that online communications would become commonplace. Anyone with a personal computer and a dial-up modem could access a bulletin board and send messages to other users. Some of these services would rapidly specialize in dating (see Figure 1.3).

Two of the BBS dating services that attracted the greatest media coverage were Dial Your Match and Matchmaker, which went online in 1981 and 1986 respectively. In addition to a place for posting "bios," they offered a matching system. New users completed an online questionnaire

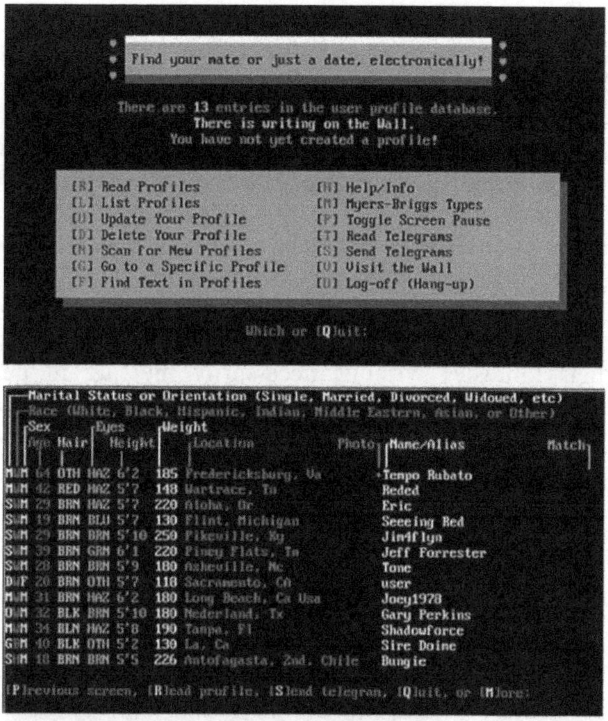

The History of Matchmaking

31

Figure 1.3. Interface of the BBS Matchmaker

with some fifty closed and open-ended questions primarily concerning sex, age, sexual orientation, physical appearance, occupation, values, hobbies, and personality. Once the form was completed, it was compared automatically with other users' responses, with the help of an algorithm programmed to find a compatible partner. Compatibility was determined by the number of identical responses, and the new user could browse through a list of "suitable" partners and send them private messages (Scharlott and Christ, 1995).

France developed a national network approximately at the same time. Users accessed a videotex system using a terminal called Minitel – a name that would ultimately come to refer to the whole network. One of the most popular features of the Minitel was that of "friendly messaging systems" (*messageries conviviales*). By the late 1980s, these chat services accounted for the lion's share of the networks' data traffic (excluding business applications), and by the mid-1990s there were some 800 platforms in France (Rincé, 1990; Jouët, 2011). The messaging services (*messageries*) were mainly operated by newspaper and magazine publishers and given names such as "Jane" and "Aline" (these two were run by the weekly *Le Nouvel Observateur*), "Turlu" (slang for telephone; run by the daily *Libération*), and "Union" (the name of an erotic magazine; run by *Hachette*). Many of them where of a sexual character. As Josiane Jouët's research shows, a lot of people used the messaging services as a forum for explicitly sexual discussions, where users could flirt and air their fantasies without necessarily meeting in person (Jouët, 1987). Although the Minitel system was not used solely for this purpose, it was to be remembered mostly for its erotic content (see Figure 1.4).

The reactions to North America's BBSs and France's *messageries* were totally different, in spite of the similarities between the two. In the United States, the growth of online communication was largely idealized and welcomed

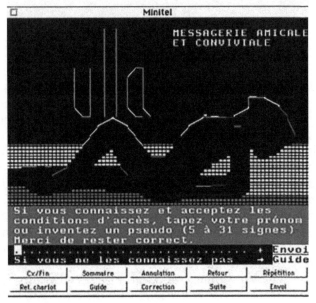

Figure 1.4. Interface of the Minitel messaging system ULLA

The History of Matchmaking 33

as a positive social change. The network's structure was seen as a horizontal universe; this is how it appeared both to its designers – academics and data scientists who were also its main users – and to the media that reported on its development (Flichy, 2001; Turner, 2010). This "digital utopianism," as Fred Turner described it, largely extended to the BBS dating services, which were also seen in a positive light. Print journalists and academics heralded BBSs as profoundly "democratic" platforms that allowed interactions to be unaffected by individuals' age, sex, social background, handicaps, or other social characteristics. Users would be able to judge each other on the basis of values, ideas, and personality rather than physical appearance, and would be freer to express their desires. The enthusiasm carried over to the explicitly sexual platforms, which were lauded for being egalitarian.

The history of the Minitel and its erotic chat services is very different. Unlike the BBSs, the Minitel was a project entirely designed, owned, and operated by the French state; and the venture was driven by a different ideology. The system was initially conceived of as a vertical broadcast information tool, which was to provide the French population with official news and services (phone book, weather broadcasts, train schedules, etc.). The state operator never envisioned the messaging services; that feature came about only because someone hacked the system. In 1982, in the eastern city of Strasbourg, the daily newspaper *Dernières Nouvelles d'Alsace* set up a local videotex news service called Gretel. Because Gretel subscribers were having trouble connecting, the newspaper's computer manager set up a chat service as a temporary way to communicate with them. Users soon hijacked the system and began communicating with one another. The newspaper declined to interfere, and this mode of communicating was an instant success. Gretel would become France's first *messagerie conviviale* (Marchand and Ancelin, 1984).

As an interactive tool grafted onto a top-down information service – and, what is more, as a tool used for a sexual purpose – the Minitel messaging was seen as "a perversion of the intrinsic rationality of the system," according to Josiane Jouët (2011). The official ideology behind the Minitel made

34 The New Laws of Love

it difficult to portray erotic chats in any positive light. A slew of highly critical books and articles denounced a new form of hedonism, caused by sexual frustration, excessive individualism, and, once again, the commodification of human relations. Whereas digital utopianism created a glowing image for North American BBSs, France's Minitel services were criticized for their double transgression – sexual and technological.

In the 1980s, a large number of governmental, academic, and business computer networks operating in the United States were gradually integrated into the "network of networks" that became the internet. Its rapid success was largely attributable to the development in the 1990s of web technologies that allowed easy access to online content. Dating sites were among the first interactive platforms to launch on the web, well before the first social media site, which appeared in 1997 (boyd and Ellison, 2007). Although a product of the web, the dating sites bore traces of earlier dating services, in relation to which they marked an evolution, not a revolution.

Old and new on the internet

In September 1995 *Wired*, then a young magazine covering technology, published an article on what it described as a company "offering an interactive digital personals service."[1] The service was Match.com, considered to be the first online dating site, and was created by Electric Classifieds Inc., a company that sold ads on the internet. Using the conventional headings of columns of classifieds in newspapers, the company launched a series of sites with the domain names Jobs.com, Autos.com, and Housing.com, as well as a separate site for dating called Match.com (Figure 1.5). As the founder explained in a 2011 interview, "[t]hat was the original idea, to do classified ads but make it electric."[2]

The concept quickly caught on. Similar sites gradually spread across North America and Europe, where they were rolled out as the internet expanded. The first investors in the new online dating market included publishers of classifieds such as Webpersonals.com, which was launched in 1997 by a company that formerly specialized in phone-based personals

The History of Matchmaking 35

Figure 1.5. Interface of Match.com (year 2000)

(Telepersonals). Other early dating sites emanated from BBSs. In 1996, the BBS-based Matchmaker migrated to the web, where it operated for two decades as Matchmaker.com. Something similar occurred in France, where some Minitel services moved to the then expanding web. The iconic *messagerie* ULLA moved to the internet in the twenty-first century, under the new name Ulla.com.

The inheritance from older services was visible in the architecture of the new platforms. Both the *messageries* and the BBSs inherited parts of their organization from agencies and personals, and passed that legacy on to the dating sites. The most striking example is the "bio," a free-text self-portrait that forms a genre in its own right, in a style used only in dating services. This specific autobiographical format was employed from the very beginning of personal ads in the nineteenth century (Garden, 2008), then moved to BBS and Minitel chat services (Fornel, 1989), and can still be found in today's online dating profiles.

The industry has since reinvented itself: nearly fifteen years after the first online dating site, the services went mobile. Applications emerged as the first generation of smartphones provided access to digital content. The first high-profile smartphone-based service was Grindr, an application launched in 2009 that targeted gay men. Mobile features included geolocation, which served to identify the user's location and to display active profiles of other users nearby. Grindr provided the template for similar apps that target heterosexuals; Blendr launched in 2011, Tinder in 2012, and the French venture Happn in 2014. Facing competition from the new mobile services and forced to adapt to a variety of devices – computers, smartphones, and tablets – the traditional sites have since moved on to develop their own mobile versions. Match, for example, is primarily accessed today through its app interface: 63% of the European users who created an account on the platform in 2019 did so by using a mobile device, and only 37% connected through the website.[3] Online dating through the web has become a minority practice, except among older users.

These apps have changed online dating to some extent. The former text-based interfaces have been superseded by visual content in which photography takes precedence over the written word. Nevertheless, today's applications, too, are descendants of earlier matchmaking services. This legacy is reflected not only in platform features (which are still based on "profiles," stated selection criteria, and written communication), but also in the identity of companies behind the applications. Tinder, for instance (Figure 1.6), first went under the name Matchbox and received initial funding from a startup incubator called Hatch Labs and financed by InterActiveCorp (IAC), a company that owns a large number of dating sites such as Match. One can say that mediated dating forms a family tree: matrimonial agencies were the first to publish personal ads; publishers of classifieds as well as BBS and Minitel operators, launched many of the earliest dating sites; and dating site companies have largely financed and developed dating apps.

But online dating sites and apps would prove far more successful than their predecessors. The extraordinary diffusion of digital practices spurred their popularity; in fact now, for the first time since the emergence of marriage brokerage, dating services are a flourishing sector of the

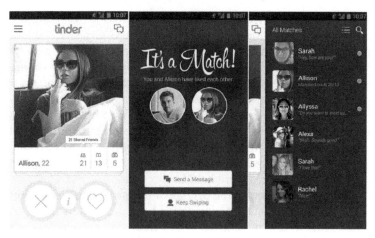

Figure 1.6. Interface of Tinder (year 2012)

economy. While early websites were built by individual entrepreneurs, the expanding market has attracted investors and has become international. Typically for growth markets, this trend is accompanied by industry consolidation. As corporations expand, they take over competitors; this creates a situation of quasi-monopoly, in which a small number of major players own most of the brands. This is the case with IAC, an internet and media conglomerate listed on Nasdaq with a portfolio of over a hundred different companies such as Match Group, which in turn owns several dating platforms – for example Match, Tinder, OkCupid, Hinge, BlackPeopleMeet, OurTime, PlentyofFish, and Meetic Group; and Meetic Group, for its part, owns Meetic, Neu, Lexa, LoveScout24, and Twoo, to mention just a few. Small fish are eaten by big fish, and big fish are eaten by giant fish – in this case, big companies are swallowed by giant corporations. In 2019 IAC reported a full-year revenue of US$4.76 billon, out of which 2.05 billion alone came from Match Group, which had seen a 19% increase from the previous year.[4]

***

Commercial matchmaking services first appeared in the nineteenth century and never fully succeeded in shaking off their shady reputation. This type of service had an inbuilt paradox: it reflected the matrimonial system of that period, but at the same time it clashed with the nascent code of romantic love, where love was depicted as blind and as a product of fate. This paradox is inherent in all dating services, as they depend upon the matching logic of their culture but are also in constant conflict with our conventional, romantic representations of love. Yet no two countries are alike: while the internet culture in the United States could reconcile online dating with the "grammar" of love, the lack of any utopia surrounding networks in France may explain why dating services were held in discredit.

The examination of the origins of online dating also shows how economic considerations have been a constant threat to the ideal of romantic love. While many of the writings on online dating consider the current situation a critical moment in the encroachment of late capitalism on the sphere of intimacy, a historical perspective indicates that the same fears have been voiced continuously throughout the twentieth and twenty-first centuries. The allegedly contemporary crisis of love epitomized by online dating turns out to be a "permanent crisis" of romantic love, to borrow a term from French anthropologist Mélanie Gourarier (2017). Rather than heralding the end of love, the assertion that marriage and committed relationships are under threat contributes to reaffirming these norms, as it is a constant reminder, to contemporaries, of what love is and is not – in other words, it is a normative assertion about what love *should be*. The indignation and the social criticism that has surrounded matchmaking services from the outset do not testify to the weakening of romantic love, but rather to the historical and continuing strength of this ideal.

2

Dating Technicians

Online dating is in many ways a morally contested market, as sites and apps are accused of turning courtship into a business (Steiner and Trespeuch, 2014; Schiller-Merkens and Balsiger, 2019). Paradoxically, these debates, which center on capitalism and on what market logic does to intimacy, make very little room, if any, for the underlying economics of the platforms in question. How is the online dating market organized, and who are the actors behind the scenes? How do the platforms operate, and what is their business model? Before turning to the issue of how online dating is changing love and sex, this chapter adopts for a moment the opposite perspective, of examining what norms and representations of dating shape these platforms and what marketing strategies characterize the businesses behind them.

A close look at the dating industry reveals a thoroughly conventional marketplace. Although dating companies attract considerable curiosity on account of their unconventional trade, the businesses themselves are hardly exceptional; this is rather a classic, textbook case of a growth market. Interviews with the founders of some of these platforms show the work that goes into making a commercial service out of dating by applying standard marketing techniques to a raw material that happens to be intimate relationships. But the entrepreneurs also imprint their personal beliefs onto this process:

The platforms they offer are shaped according to their own notions of love, intimacy, sex, and gender. The online dating landscape is mapped out by IT professionals and tech entrepreneurs – overwhelmingly heterosexual men who invented the mechanisms. The present chapter opens the doors to this male-dominated factory of dating platforms that is structured by three fundamental principles: copying, segmenting, and investing in stereotypes.

Copy and paste

The internet boom in the early part of the decade 2000–2010 saw a proliferation of tech companies in the western world. The digital economy was growing fast and bolstered the idea that there was easy money to be made online. The internet seemed to announce an Alaska gold rush that was promising riches to early movers, and start-ups flooded the market. European entrepreneurs looked to the United States and tried to import business models that had already succeeded overseas. The German site Alando, for instance, was launched in 1999 as a carbon copy of the American auction site eBay, while the French CaraMail was closely modeled on Hotmail and soon became one of the largest webmail platforms in France.

The same happened in online dating. By 2003, it was estimated that dating sites generated profits of over $400 million in the United States, which made them the highest-earning sector in terms of online content spending.[1] Around the same time, national dating sites popped up all around Europe: the German dating site Parship.de went online on Saint-Valentine's day in 2001, being followed by the Swedish Mötesplatsen.se the same year and, later, by the French Meetic.fr and the Dutch Lexa.nl, both launched in 2002. Far from developing new concepts for their domestic market, the European entrepreneurs launched sites that were virtually identical with the American originals. Interviews with the founders of some of the earliest French dating sites reveal the extent to which copying dominated the industry. French pioneer sites such as Netclub.fr and Meetic.fr were duly copied from the Match.com model,

Dating Technicians   *41*

and in turn became a template for the rest of the domestic market to follow.

> I didn't reinvent the wheel. I said to myself: there are people who have already thought this through. There were four people running Netclub at the time. I thought to myself that they'd thought through how to do it. The site works well, is appealing and user-friendly. We'll try to do the same thing. (Nicolas, 38, founder of a mainstream dating site launched in 2000)

> CÉDRIC: People often say "your dating site looks like Meetic." It's kind of true, there are standards to follow you know, in terms of home page layout...
> FARID: ...that Meetic itself took from Match.
> CÉDRIC: Yes, it's true that there are standards of layout that Match and eHarmony have imposed since ten years ago. (Cédric and Farid, both 36, founders of a niche dating site launched in 2006)

Copying existing models is not restricted to dating sites; it is a common business practice observed in many sectors of the economy. Paul DiMaggio and Walter Powell used the term "mimetic isomorphism" to describe the tendency to imitate competitors that leads to standardization of products and services (DiMaggio and Powell, 1983). Through a self-reinforcing process, models established by industry pioneers gradually become standards when new players enter a market and must find ways of dealing with established norms of production.

Dating sites are a textbook case of this product homogenization (see Figure 2.1). CEOs pay close attention to competitors and copy the design and architecture of existing products whenever possible. Far from venturing off the beaten track, they aim to benefit from the existing state of the art: "We didn't go against the tide; we managed to catch the right wave" (Mathieu, 33, founder of a mainstream site and of several niche sites). The same process was at work when mobile apps appeared (see Figure 2.1). The market leaders in the United States, especially Tinder, provided the template for European entrepreneurs to copy. Mobile apps ended up having so much in common that they can easily be

Figure 2.1. Homogeneity in dating app interfaces: from left to right, Tinder, Bumble, Hinge, happn, and Facebook Dating

confused: a large-scale photo; name and age at the bottom of the screen; a button for "liking" the profile (typically in the shape of a heart); and two other buttons, for liking or writing to the user. As the new players walk in the footsteps of the pioneers, the operating principles are established early on and rarely revisited. A Swiss research team showed that this replication of design and functionalities is favored by the agglomeration of brands, as sister companies in a same business (such as the platforms owned by Match Group) borrow programming technics from one another, and "the practice of reusing code and assembling components is common among programmers" (Pidoux et al., 2021, p. 19).

What makes mimetic isomorphism all the stronger is that many dating entrepreneurs do not claim to have any special knowledge of intimate relationships or couple formation. They tend to play it safe, by fine-tuning existing models rather than coming up with new concepts. What brings them to online dating is an interest, not in matchmaking, but in the tech industry. Several people whom I interviewed in this research stressed the arbitrary nature of their occupational choice, as they could just as well have come up with an entirely different type of site or app:

> I said to myself: "I made a carpooling site that doesn't work that well, I have the know-how to do websites, why wouldn't I make a dating site? [...] The advantage is that technically it's the same thing." (Nicolas, 38, founder of a mainstream dating site launched in 2000)

We decided to do a consumer app, and we went through all possible types of consumer apps, each time trying to figure out if there was something we could do. We thought first of doing a social network app around sport, but we got stuck in the brainstorming about that, so we moved on to the next idea, and that's how we ended up doing dating. (Simon and Patrick, both 31, founders of a mainstream dating app launched in 2019)

Most of the dating entrepreneurs have a background in technology, digital design, or management and focus primarily on the technical expertise or financial features of their business. When asked about the logic of dating, many of them readily admit to be clueless on the matter. This denial of expertise distinguishes them from most occupational groups, which claim special skills or know-how in their fields. Advisors in matrimonial agencies, for example, largely advertise their specialized know-how in matchmaking. Another insightful comparison comes from an apparently unrelated industry: pornography. In his research on the French porn industry, sociologist Mathieu Trachman reports on how the directors downplay the technical skills required to make a porn movie, on the grounds that anyone can hold a camera, while they boast of "sexual skills that set them apart from ordinary heterosexuals" (Trachman, 2013, p. 13). Entrepreneurs in dating say exactly the opposite. While dismissing the usefulness of any special knowledge in the area of dating, they insist on the need for technical expertise for anyone who wants to be successful in their domain. They identify first and foremost as "tech" people and like to present themselves as mere dating technicians. This vision of their occupation was aptly conveyed by the founder of Meetic, Marc Simoncini, who questioned the need for any specific skills in managing a company in his market area:

JOURNALIST: Meetic has become a social phenomenon. Has that transformed you into a sociologist or an analyst of the contemporary world? [...] Has it changed you, or not? You're a matchmaker!

MARC SIMONCINI: Yes, but that wasn't my aim at the time. What I do is internet. I approached Meetic as a pretty tremendous business model. And since then I've been

44 The New Laws of Love

asked so many questions about relations between men and women. Look, the first question [in the program] was how do Swedish people meet. How should I know how they meet? [...]

JOURNALIST: What's surprising is that one would expect you to have an anthropologist or a sociologist in the building, someone who wouldn't cost too much, to analyze all this and potentially help you to evolve or to interpret all the data. But the real surprise, at the end of the day, is that it runs itself.

MARC SIMONCINI: Yes, exactly! You have to remember that Meetic is simply a tool. What I found was a platform that people really liked for meeting other people. It's not me who makes Meetic what it is. Meetic is nothing; Meetic is just the people who are on it. (Radio interview with Marc Simoncini, FranceInfo, June 19, 2010)

In this radio interview Simoncini is repeatedly questioned about expertise in matchmaking, something the journalist imagines to be the company's core competency. Because he is in the business of online dating, shouldn't he be a specialist? How can the service operate if it "runs itself," without any expert at the controls? The interviewee's annoyance is evident from the recording; he argues that no special knowledge is required for a dating site. As CEO, he does not intervene in the service; he presents it as a self-managed platform.

Simoncini's confession of ignorance is not entirely disingenuous. Among the entrepreneurs interviewed for this project, rare are those who are interested in research on dating, who conduct or pay for studies on the topic, or who do in-depth analysis of "all the data," as the journalist here suggests. They readily admit that they neither know nor seek to know what people actually do on their platforms. The common thread running through their discourse (in interviews with the press as well as in front of a curious sociologist) is that they merely provide a platform for interactions over which they exercise no control.

This line of reasoning is a marketing argument. To insist on lack of interference in online dating serves the purpose of promoting a product in harmony with the romantic ideal of fate, according to which future partners meet without any third-party intervention. It also expresses an ideology according to which digital platforms are online "communities," that is, horizontal self-managed networks that are merely the sum of their users. Unlike marriage advisors in agencies, who seek to embody their business and its know-how, founders of dating platforms try to go unnoticed. Interestingly, their professional pride does not stem from any knowledge of dating, but rather from their presumed ignorance on this matter. This denial of expertise is put at the very core of the industry: because these are high-tech entrepreneurs, their products presumably have nothing to do with older and discredited forms of matchmaking services.

Market segmentation

Online dating services are not only highly standardized; they are also segmented. Users are targeted and differentiated according to multiple criteria, for example age (senior dating), race (black, Arab, Latinx, or Asian dating), religion (Jewish, Christian, or Muslim dating), and social class ("elite," "VIP," or "quality" dating). This segmentation has characterized online dating from the outset. In the United States, platforms targeting Christian or Afro-American populations were launched already in the 1990s (Coleman and Bahnan, 2008) and, before them, several bulletin board systems (BBSs) already specialized in "niche dating" (Scharlott and Christ, 1995).

Whereas in North America this market segmentation is considered part and parcel of a multicultural society, it has had bad press in some European countries. In France particularly, where universalism is a strong political discourse, niche brands have been depicted as a shift toward ethnic separatism. Dating sites and apps targeting Muslims or Arabs attract particular attention. As they are CEOs of a dating platform for individuals who come from the Maghreb, Farid and Cédric can vouch for this phenomenon:

> The media see us as a communitarian site. People don't seek to understand, they say "oh it's a religious site" and then you fall into all types of clichés about the suburb, religion etc. For example, there was an article in *Le Monde,* which was

46 The New Laws of Love

> in substance OK, but the photo of us was entitled "Suburban business." (Cédric, 36)

With hundreds of thousands of users, this ethnic dating site was said by the journalist in question to be "surfing on a communitarian wave."[2] In reality, the multiplication of targeted platforms is primarily a marketing strategy. Faced with an existing market dominated by a small number of players, new entrants seek to differentiate among consumers in order to occupy specific market segments. The dating entrepreneurs are the first to recognize this: "You have to look at it from an economics perspective, or an entrepreneur's right. You tend to do a lot better if you create some focus [...] and the more you can take people to that specific idea right from the get-go, the more you can charge them" (Ben, 41, founder of a niche dating site). To earn their place in the market, many businesses shift from *direct* competition with the big mainstream platforms to *lateral* competition, by concentrating on a segment (Bourdieu, 1997). The transition from mass to niche is a familiar strategy in the marketing literature, and one that guides many online dating entrepreneurs.

> As far as the [platform's] image is concerned, you have to choose your positioning. Today, if you want to go in as a mainstream dating site for the general public, good luck, it's already crowded. You'd have to get up early and wait years before really taking off and having a worthwhile set of registered users. That's why I think it's easier today to position yourself in a niche, you know, it could be seniors or anything, whatever you want. (Mathieu, 33, founder of a mainstream senior black gay and lesbian dating platform)

The result of this market segmentation can be a dizzying proliferation of dating services, some more narrowly targeted than others, that promise matches for "geeks" (Dragon Fruit App), outdoor enthusiasts (LuvByrd), Trump voters (Righter) or fitness fans (Datefit). By the time this book is published, some of these apps will probably have ceased to exist. Many niche platforms are short-lived, as they fail to find an audience. This is because the entrepreneurs think in terms of "business concepts" rather than social groups and communities, and many apps and sites do not resonate with any known homogamous mechanism. Only those that do, for instance platforms based on social, racial, or religious homophily, make it in the long run. All others contribute to the high failure rate of dating sites and apps.

This profusion of differentiated products is not specific to online dating but characterizes most contemporary markets, in which the "average consumer" has been replaced by a multitude of lifestyle brands. A similar trend is at work in the pornography industry. Whereas early films had fairly similar scripts as far as actors and sexual practices go, the turn to the web increased the diversity in pornographic content through numerous niches and "tags" that feature fantasies for specific audiences (Trachman, 2013; Mazières et al., 2014). The result is an inflation of novelties. As media specialist David Hesmondhalgh shows, cultural industries are characterized by an "overproduction" where misses are offset against hits. The aim is to launch many different products or brands in order to determine *retrospectively* what works: it's like "'throwing mud' – or other similar substances – 'against the wall' to see what sticks" (Hesmondhalgh, 2012, p. 30).

Segmentation is fully consistent with the high degree of standardization. The founders of niche services show the same copying tendencies as the rest of the industry: far from proposing customized spaces, they offer platforms with such a strong resemblance to mainstream services that in many cases the only clue to the audience they target is the product name and the pictures put for display (e.g. black dating sites have no specificities other than using the word "black" in the name and putting photos of black people on the home page). In other words, the target has no effect on the platform features:

> There's nothing specific. It's always the same platform anyway. Look at it this way: we're in the age of Fordism. [...] When Renault makes its Mégane model, they reuse the same frame for other cars. [...] So we release one platform, and then we duplicate it. (Mathieu, 33, founder of mainstream, senior, black, gay and lesbian dating platforms)

The copying goes even further for specialized services, as founders typically invest in niches that have already been

48 The New Laws of Love

invented by others. It is not uncommon for a niche concept to be exploited in North America before being imported in Europe and rolled out by a number of companies. A case in point is that of extramarital dating sites, which have multiplied in the latter part of the decade 2000–2010. The first platform to offer "an affair" was AshleyMadison, launched in the United States and Canada in 2002. The concept was quickly borrowed by others – hence the French company Gleeden. In an interview with members of the management team of Gleeden, the press officer readily acknowledged that the service was largely modeled on its North American counterpart and was launched opportunistically, to fill a market gap. The founders, she said, "wanted to launch a dating site in France and wondered what hadn't been done before" (Sarah, 27). Whereas only one extramarital dating site was registered in France before the highly publicized launch of Gleeden, tens of them went online in the following years. Rather than a sign of the rise in infidelity, as is often claimed,[3] these ventures are a perfect illustration of a marketing technique that comes straight from a manual.

A clean, well-lighted place

In her sharp essay on love and sex in the digital era, the American journalist Emily Witt pins down the philosophy of Tinder in one phrase: "its success with straight people had everything to do with changing Grindr into 'a clean, well-lighted space'" (Witt, 2016, p. 28). With this expression, borrowed from a book by Ernest Hemingway, she perfectly describes the proper, almost sterile universe of mainstream dating platforms. I had the opportunity to study and quantify this phenomenon in 2008, when I conducted a systematic analysis of 218 French dating websites (Bergström, 2011a, 2011b). What I found was a market fundamentally structured by a stereotypical opposition between *sex* and *love*. Mainstream dating sites promote themselves as "serious" platforms that foster marriage and romantic relationships. This wholesome image is aimed at marking the difference from another type of platforms, which promote hookups, casual sex, or extramarital affairs and make a business out of being sexually transgressive.

This antagonistic marketing results in two very different kinds of platforms, each with its own distinctive color schemes and imagery (see Figure 2.2). The analysis showed that the so-called "serious" dating sites predominantly used crisp, clear colors with a preference for white, blue and grey. Logos often added a touch of pink or red and invoked symbols of love or passion – hearts, arrows, and flames. The sexual dating sites were built with much warmer, darker shades – primarily black, red, purple, and pink – and often displayed conventional symbols of temptation such as devils, carnival masks, and the apple of Eden. The same contrasts were evident in the photographs that companies used on their homepage. The "serious" services showed smiling, brown-haired couples in light-colored clothes where the woman was often placed behind the man, in an embrace that (in a heteronormative context) cannot be misinterpreted as sexual. The sexual dating sites preferred to feature individual women – often blondes or redheads – showing far more skin (Bergström, 2011a, 2011b).

These stylized universes are immediately recognizable; they present the same type of stereotypes as those used in publicity. Dating companies make extensive use of advertising strategies, identified by sociologist Erwin Goffman as "the use of scenes and characters which have come to be stereotypically identified with a particular kind of activity by the widest range of viewers, thus ensuring instantaneous recognizability" (Goffman, 1979, p. 26). Dating companies make no attempt to be subtle. Using symbols that are unequivocal and universally intelligible, they are ready to

Figure 2.2. Stereotypical branding between love and sex (Match and EasyFlirt)

50 The New Laws of Love

embrace clichés to differentiate their platforms. Colors, photographs, and logos are all chosen to position the products on offer within a specific symbolic universe – either *sex* or *love*.

Creators of dating apps like to think they changed the game. Mobile apps are said to have revolutionized the dating culture, tuning it to modern norms and to young people who are "single, not sorry," to quote the 2019 Tinder publicity campaign. A glimpse at the features and general image of the mainstream dating apps makes it clear, however, that they, too, are extremely proper and restrained as far as sexual matters are concerned. The publicity talks of dating, love and even friendship but never of sex. Tinder is commonly associated with hookups, but – probably because of this – it is marketed as a "social network" no less than as a dating app, and sexual allusions are strictly banned from the official communication. In an infamous interview with the *Evening Standard*, the Tinder CEO Sean Rad made an effort to persuade the journalist that he was a "romantic," someone "ready to settle down" and have "lots of children" and "desperate to impress on [her] how gallant he is."[4] The interview was the talk of the town: Rad went off script, talking about his sexual experience, and confused *sapiosexual* with *sodomy*. The head of marketing and communication, who was present during the interview, had an outburst – "That's it! We're going to be fired" – and the Match Group company officially disavowed the interview.[5]

Part of this prude image is due to the strict policies that regulate mobile apps. App Store proscribes "overtly sexual or pornographic material [...] intended to stimulate erotic rather than aesthetic or emotional feelings";[6] in much the same way, Google Play accepts nudity only "if the primary purpose is educational, documentary, scientific or artistic, and is not gratuitous."[7] For the numerous dating apps using Facebook Login to access the platform, this sexual censorship is redoubled by the social network's strict ban on all types of "objectionable content" (starting with female nipples). But this is not the whole picture. The prude image of mainstream apps is less about imposed restrictions than about their heterosexual target group. On gay platforms such as Grindr, Hornet, and Scruff, users may provide graphic descriptions

Dating Technicians

of their bodies, preferred sex positions ("top," "bottom," or "versatile"), and other sexual preferences. Although profile photos cannot be explicit, the chat system allows for both videos and photos with sexual content to be sent. That is a far cry from apps that mainly target a heterosexual audience where the search for sex can be communicated only between the lines. However, this straight policy is not truly aimed at hindering hookups, or even at creating distictions between "serious" and "casual" dating. Preserving a clean *image* is paramount:

> JULIEN: I wanted a very clean image – but then people do whatever they want on the other side. But a very clean image [...]
> INTERVIEWER: What do you mean by "clean?"
> JULIEN: I mean that whatever consenting adults do outside the site is none of our business. Everything they do inside the site is said and done between the lines. (Julien, 32, founder of a mainstream dating site)

The term "clean" runs like a leitmotif through my interviews with dating entrepreneurs; it is used to designate platforms that display a virtuous interface. As Julien points out, what matters here is the image projected by the platform rather than how it is actually used. According to another founder, "it's like a car. You give people a car, a BMW, they might drive fast or they might not, it's the driver that decides [...] we give them a framework" (Mathieu, 33). Uninterested in what people actually do, the founders are primarily concerned with the platforms reputation. This prudent marketing has a clear target: women.

Gender stereotyping

As much as they draw upon a stereotypical opposition between sex and love, dating platforms also rely on a traditional vision of male and female sexuality. As one of the entrepreneurs puts it, "men are from Mars; women are from Venus; they want different things" (Ben, 41). Many of the interviewees embrace a conventional distinction between men's sexuality, portrayed as self-centered and driven by a high libido, and women's sexuality, which is seen as relational and more prude. This is how the "clean" image of mainstream platforms targets primarily women:

> Women are very important to us. It's this serious mainstream positioning. It's for serious dating. Here you're not going to get... the penis length of the person that's talking to you [information that appears on certain gay platforms]. No, the idea is that you're going to be able to make something of your life, you know. Well, we try to prioritize meeting women's needs. (Mathieu, 33, founder of a mainstream site and of several niche sites)

Dating companies develop wholesome platforms in an attempt to appeal to women, whom (male) entrepreneurs consider to be a "difficult" audience. To gain trust, many platforms market themselves as designed "by women" or "for women," and many businesses put forth their female press managers rather than their male CEOs. This marketing strategy is based on the underlying idea that female sexuality is complex, even mysterious, and involves special needs that must be addressed. The rather allusive answers I received to questions about what these needs may look like make me believe that this strategy is partly defensive: because they are uncertain about what women "really want," the entrepreneurs steer clear of anything that could possibly give offense.

This prudent approach is even more pronounced in the case of lesbian platforms. By comparison to gay apps and dating sites, platforms for bisexual and homosexual women are astonishingly few. Those that do exist are often presented as "communities" or "social networks," where the sexual and romantic dimension is tuned down, or even absent. Contrary to what is sometimes said,[8] the explanation for this is not that lesbians shy away from online dating; in fact lesbian women are far more frequent users of dating apps than straight women are (see chapter 3). The reason is rather that tech companies are predominantly male workplaces and, while dating entrepreneurs regard women as a "difficult" audience, all-female platforms are considered particularly "risky." In her interviews with the press, Robyn Exton, CEO of the queer and lesbian dating app HER, stresses her difficulties in obtaining funding for her business "because many investors don't see queer women as a profitable demographic."[9] The small number of lesbian platforms, the reluctance to invest in those that exist, and their orientation toward friendship rather than dating show how hard it is for certain entrepreneurs and investors to address what lesbian relationships might look like, or even to imagine any sexuality in the absence of a man.

To the extent that the "serious" or even friendly image is aimed at women, explicitly sexual platforms target men. This is the case of gay apps and sites that often have a sexually explicit image. More unexpected, however, is the discovery that this also applies to the heterosexual platforms promoting hookups or casual sex (e.g. apps like Wild, HUD, or DOWN). The entrepreneurs I interviewed think that this type of services targets only men:

> It's a product called Sexy [= modified name] but that's no longer for dating, because it's pure fantasy. In other words, it's people talking with each other about sex, but they never exchange phone numbers; nothing real ever happens. We suspect that most of the women on it are really men pretending to be lesbians and talking to other men also pretending to be lesbians. Well, it's all very complicated. [...] Basically it's a discharge of desire for men. (Grégoire, 46, founder of a sexual dating site)

Many hookup apps and casual dating sites are intended for a male audience, as platforms for fantasy fulfillment. As another founder put it, these are services where "men come and want to look at certain pictures" (Ben, 41). Although posing as dating platforms, they constitute more of a novel genre of pornographic service, which caters for male fantasies about "the girl next door" – a figure readily available for sex. When the media discover – typically after a platform has been hacked, as AshleyMadison was in July 2015 – that most users are males and that the "female" profiles are fakes or "bots," the dating entrepreneurs are the last ones to be surprised, although some of them certainly regret that the tricks of the trade have been revealed.

> Hookup platforms... Let me tell you, I don't have the numbers, but for certain, 95% of the hookup platforms are

54   The New Laws of Love

scam. (Mathieu, 33, founder of a mainstream site and of other niche sites)

[If you look at] sites in that kind of business, where you see hookups and one-night stands, in any case, for me – I don't know, but I can't really see women saying: "Hey, I'm going to register for a one-night stand." That doesn't exist. Well, it must exist somewhere, but we also know what sorts of things are going on behind all that, on those sites. It's mostly men who are going to register. That's 95% and, out of the remaining 5%, 2.5% are prostitutes looking for work, and then, at night, maybe 2.5% of French nymphomaniacs. (Farid, 36, founder of a niche dating site)

In other words, serious dating is for women, while casual sex is for men… Digital technology might have reinvented modern dating, but the apps and sites prove to be a stubbornly conventional invention, organized around the stereotypical opposition between sex (associated with men) and love (associated with women). The causal mechanisms at work here are many and bidirectional. While it is true that women are often more sexually reserved than men (we will come back to this in chapter 7 and try to understand why), dating platforms exaggerate these differences and capitalize on them. They routinely exploit gender stereotypes and thereby participate in reproducing them. Many hookup apps have a sexually aggressive image, which in their marketing clearly targets a male audience; and these apps do indeed have few female users. Thus the entrepreneurs have created their own self-fulfilling prophecy.

It's a man's world

It's no different from the night club owner in Paris; they have a ladies' night for a reason. You know, men don't want to come to what we call, don't be offended, a sausage fest. You don't want to walk into a bar and pay for bottle service if all you're looking at is a bunch of other men; then you just go to a football match. Right. What you wanna walk into is a room full of pretty women. That's just how the world works. Right. That's what men want. So, there is no point spending all your time on a service where they are greatly outnumbering the women. It won't be buyable. (Ben, 41, founder of a niche dating site)

The message is perfectly clear: the customer base for dating sites and apps is primarily male. Ben is the founder of a large North American platform available in many different countries. He drew an analogy with nightclubs in order to answer my questions about the business of online dating and explain to me why the only paying customers on his site and on numerous other sites are men. Many platforms, whether they charge for membership or for additional features, waive charges for women. Even when both sexes are required to pay, there are often ways for women to be exempted. Freemium models too are often based on a gendered economics. The real-time bidding that characterizes today's digital ad auctions (where companies bid to have their advertisement instantly displayed online) leads many dating platforms to pay more for women than for men. In other words, when the male users don't pay for accessing women, the companies do.

By and large, online dating is a man's world. The CEOs are, typically, men who target male customers and strive to provide "what men want" – namely, in Ben's male banter, "a room full of pretty women." The business model is one in which women resemble the service being offered. Much as dating entrepreneurs strive to offer services that appeal to women – something to make women "comfortable" and "confident," in their own language – they openly admit that women are a means much more than they are an end:

> INTERVIEWER: You said the site is designed for women. Why is it important to adapt to women?
> CHRISTOPHE: Because, whatever happens, if there are women on the site, the men will come as well [...] so we have to find a way to cater to them. (Christophe, 29, founder of a niche dating site)

Women must be catered for in order to attract men – the paying customers. The business model of online dating platforms, in which males assume the financial burden, is consistent with what the Italian anthropologist Paola Tabet describes as a sexual–economic exchange – the exchange that governs heterosexual relationships (Tabet, 2004). Men

The New Laws of Love

paying to date women is not a scenario limited to the digital world. Paying for drinks, meals, flowers, cinema tickets, and the like is, by tradition, incumbent on the male partner in dating. Although thought of as *gifts*, these objects form part of an exchange in which the counter-gift is access to women's sexuality. What is more, as Paola Tabet explains, gifts are evidence of the difference in the status assigned to female and male sexuality.

> Inequality within sexuality itself is affirmed and secured by gift–payment. In other words, the gift implies and constantly imposes a difference between the sexual subjects. For the recipient, it implies a renunciation, if only partial, of that person's sexual needs and desires. In this respect, the gift speaks the language of domination. The mere fact of giving, systematically (or more or less systematically), in exchange for the sexual act of another person, not only one's own sexual act but also a gift supposes that one fails to recognize the same urgency, the same necessity, and the same autonomy in the other person's sexuality. (Tabet, 2004, p. 55)

The idea implicit in the gift is that women are less willing than men to engage in sexual relations, or that they give in or renounce something when they do so, and therefore need to be encouraged or rewarded for it. The same logic is at work in the economics of online dating services. Waiving payment for women, or spending more on advertising for them, is predicated on the idea that women are somehow less interested in dating online or less willing to engage in it, and must therefore be incentivized to sign up. By the same token, however, because they are no longer (paying) customers, they become assimilated to the services on offer. Like other gifts, free online dating access presupposes, and therefore imposes, as Tabet puts it, a "difference between sexual subjects" (p. 55). The online dating business model is predicated on the unequal status between women and men in heterosexual exchanges and on catering for that inequality.

* * *

When trying to figure out how online dating works, we tend to scrutinize the platforms in an attempt to detect user behavior. It's easy to jump to the conclusion that, by observing the technical features, we can uncover new romantic and sexual norms. In reality, how the platforms operate tells us more about marketing and economic norms than about usage. Market conventions are often established in the absence of any customer; when conceiving their offer, founders and CEOs of course anticipate the "demand," but they must also conform to the customs and considerations specific of their industry, when it comes to technology and business plans. If these platforms convey a "philosophy" of online dating, as some observers claim (Parmentier, 2012) it is not an abstract philosophy, but one crafted by and embodied in these tech entrepreneurs.

In other words, we cannot consider the production side and the reception side of online dating as two aspects of the same phenomenon. The market has a certain autonomy and follows its own logic, even when businesses claim simply to be meeting customer demand. Conversely, usage is framed by the platforms, but never determined by the technical features or the marketing logic. The growing interconnection between intimacy and economy invites us to be attentive to their respective mechanisms rather than to see them as simply two sides of the same coin.

3

The Keys to Success

Why has online dating been so successful, and how does it continue to attract so many users? The expanding role of the internet in our lives tells only a part of the story, and is less important than the underlying social conditions. After examining the history and the industry of online dating in the first two chapters, we turn now to users. The chapter reviews the circumstances that have made the hitherto discredited recourse to intermediaries so popular today, and focuses on the extraordinary transformations that have affected love and sexuality in recent decades.

A glance at the rearview mirror shows how far things have changed. Well into the 1950s, sexuality, conjugality, and marriage largely coincided; since then their autonomy has increased. Today the first sexual partner rarely becomes the first life partner: between these two stages there is now a period of sexual experimentation, during which women and men are initiated into matters of intimacy without yet thinking about settling down. Similarly, the first life partner is no longer necessarily the only one. Separation has become a common experience and is often followed by repartnering, even at relatively advanced ages.

Online dating owes its success to the new complexity of these trajectories and corresponds to issues that are specific to a certain age group. It appeals first and foremost to young people, whom it offers platforms for sexual exploration, which is favored by the characteristic discretion of digital dating. Among older adults, the increase in the use of these services is accounted for by the possibility they create to seek a partner outside one's social circle. At an age at which social life often becomes limited, dating platforms become an important means of (re)partnering, especially at a stage in life when the shortage of singles is a demographic fact. In both cases, the key to success lies on the one hand in structural changes, that is, in the profound transformation of intimate life, and on the other hand in the specificity of these platforms, namely in the private nature of online dating.

How big is online dating?

How big is online dating really? In recent years, multiple figures have been brandished regarding app users and the proportion of couples that start off this way. Numbers are generally striking and are often presented by the stakeholders themselves: apps and websites claim hundreds of thousands of users across the world. Tinder's CEO asserted in a 2020 interview that the app had been downloaded more than 340 million times since its launch in 2012.[1] But what does this figure represent? How common is online dating in the general population? Only surveys can answer these questions, as they collect data on both users and non-users. The next two sections present results from rigorous scientific surveys that tell us how important online dating is, how many couples meet this way, and who those who seek partners online are.

Providing a panorama of online dating around the world is not an easy task. Scientific surveys on the topic are scarce, sometimes old, and reliable data are rare outside the West. Another challenge lies in making comparisons between countries. Strictly speaking, surveys are rarely comparable: differences in sampling, design, questions, scope, and timing make cross-country analysis difficult. The main tendency is, however, clear. In all countries where data are available we see a clear rise in the use of online dating platforms over time, albeit at different rates. Figure 3.1 shows how usage has evolved in France, the United States, and Germany.

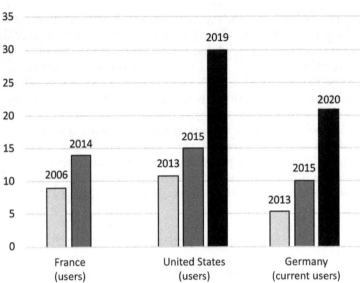

Figure 3.1. Rate of use of online dating platforms in France, the United States, and Germany (%)

France Scope: all individuals aged 26–65; Question: Have you ever used a dating website?

US Scope: all individuals aged 18+; Question: Have you ever used a dating website or app?

Germany Scope: currently single individuals born in the periods 1971–3, 1981–3, or 1991–3; Question: Are you currently using a dating website (2013, 2015, 2020) or an app (2020)?

SOURCES: CSF survey (France, 2006, INSERM–INED), EPIC survey (France, 2013–14, INED-INSEE), IALP survey (US, 2013, Pew Research Center), PTS survey (US, 2015, Pew Research Center), ATP survey, wave 56 (US, 2019, Pew Research Center), Pairfam survey, waves 5, 7 and 12 (Germany, 2012–13, 2014–15, 2019–20, DFG).

Although the surveys were carried out at different points in time and with different methodologies, they give us a hint of the progressive spread of digital matchmaking.

In France, online dating took on surprisingly quickly. In the early years of the decade 2000–2010, as the country still held on to its national Minitel network, comparatively few households were connected to the World Wide Web.[2] Despite this, 9% of the French population aged between 26 and 65 years had already used an online dating website by 2006. In

2014, the rate had risen to 14%. Figures for the United States are more recent. US surveys carried out by the Pew Research Center reveal that, in 2019, 30% of American adults had already used an online dating site or app. This is a steep rise by comparison with earlier figures. In 2013 the share was only 11%; it rose to 15% in 2015. This means that usage almost tripled in the United States in only six years.

The study of online dating is framed differently in Germany. A large longitudinal survey regularly asks German panelists about their private and family life. Singles are asked whether they are *currently* using an online dating site or app, "to flirt or to look for a partner." Whereas in 2013 only 5% of these respondents, aged 19 to 42 at the time, declared using a dating site, by 2020 the proportion of members of this same group, now seven years older, who used either an app or a site had gone up to 21%.

This makes online dating historically unique. Unlike former matchmaking services, which never made it to the general public (see chapter 1), this new type of intermediaries has generated a fairly common way of meeting partners and is now even an integral part of a single's experience. But high-rising numbers are far from saying that everyone goes online. The fact that almost a third of the US population has used a dating platform still means that two thirds (70%) *have not*. These proportions are important to keep in mind.

Indeed, there is always a risk of overestimating online dating. Since sensational figures make for better press, journalists and even scientists are inclined to present astonishing figures. The risk of exaggeration is even higher when we attempt to understand how many couples meet this way. Some surveys tend to boost the results. By using an extensive definition of "online dating" – say, one that includes all the encounters that involve chatting, messaging, or getting to know someone in any type of online setting – or by adopting a very broad understanding of "relationship" – one that runs from "more than holding hands" to being married – you can easily end up with mind-boggling statistics. With more strict methods and precise definitions, the results are less overwhelming, maybe more trivial, but also much more accurate. What does an analysis carried out on stricter principles reveal?

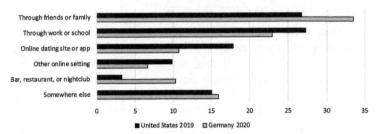

Figure 3.2. Ranking of meeting venues in the United States in 2019 and in Germany in 2020 (%)

Scope US: 18+-year-olds, married or in a committed relationship, who met their current partner less than three years before the survey.

Scope Germany: 26–49-year-olds in a relationship, who met their current partner less than 3 years before the survey.

Sources: ATP survey, wave 56 (US, 2019, Pew Research Center), Pairfam survey, waves 10 to 12 (Germany, 2017–2020, DFG).

I will focus here on the United States and Germany (Figure 3.2), where figures are most recent. In the United States, online dating is today the third most common way of meeting a spouse: in 2019, 18% of American adults living in marriage or in a committed relationship formed during the previous three years had met their partner on a dating site or app. This ranks online dating third among US meeting venues, after family or friends (27%) and work or school (27%): it is more common than both other online settings (10%) and in-person settings such as bars or restaurants (3%). The results are similar for Germany. In 2020, among individuals who met their current spouse less than three years before the survey, online dating apps and sites ranked third as well (11%). It lagged far behind meetings through relatives, friends, or acquaintances (34%) and through work or school (23%),[3] but came close to meetings in a bar or a nightclub (10%) and was more common than other online settings (7%).

Who seeks love and sex online?

The overall statistics on rates of use tells us nothing about who these users are. But this is important, because individuals

The Keys to Success   63

who resort to dating platforms are actually a minority, as are couples that meet through these platforms.

A striking result across many countries is the high prevalence of online dating in the LGBT population (Rosenfeld and Thomas, 2012; Bergström, 2016b). App and site users are, first and foremost, gay and lesbian users. In the United States, more than a half of bisexual and homosexual men and women declare having used an app or a site (55%, versus 28% among those who identify as straight).[4] This is not something entirely new, as gays and lesbians are, historically, big users of matchmaking services – a trend that the internet has accentuated.

Class differences in online dating were strong in the early days of the internet but have become less pronounced over time. With the spread of internet connectivity, computers, and smartphones, the "digital divide" in online dating is shrinking. But trends differ across countries, and results depend on whether we consider the proportion of users or the proportion of couples that meet this way. In Germany, for instance, there are educational differences when it comes to singles who *currently* use a dating site or app. The proportion of users increases with educational attainment.[5] In the United States, too, more educated individuals are more likely to have used dating sites and apps at least once, but these educational differences tend to create a contrast en bloc between individuals with no more than a high-school degree and people with higher education. In other words, a specific degree does not predict usage rate in the United States, it's the fact of having been to university that comes with a higher probability of using a dating platform.[6]

Interestingly, tendencies are different when it comes to the couples formed through online dating. In Germany, no clear educational differences can be found between these couples and individuals who met elsewhere. But in the United States couples formed through online dating are much more educated than couples formed in other settings. This means that, while in Germany it's the fact of using a dating app that is socially differentiated, in the United States it is rather the fact of finding a spouse this way that differs across educational groups.[7] Finally, it should be noted that no differences can be established in relation to race: in the United States

64 The New Laws of Love

we find comparable numbers of black, white, and Hispanic individuals who declare using online dating services, and the differences between them with regard to meeting one's spouse this way are not statistically significant.[8]

Apart from sexual orientation, the one variable that stands out as a fundamental characteristic in online dating is age. Young people are by far those who use online dating sites and apps the most. The United States serves once more as a good example: in 2019, 48% of the Americans aged between 18 and 29 had used such a platform, versus 13% of those aged 65 or older.[9] The trend is the same in other countries. However, young people do not necessarily form couples this way. A striking and intriguing pattern is that, although people aged 29 or younger are the main *users* of online dating services, older people more commonly *find a spouse* this way. In France, Germany, and the United States, couples formed through online dating are predominantly repartnered unions between older people (Bergström 2016b; Danielsbacka et al., 2020; Lampard, 2020).

The contradiction is merely apparent. It suggests a fundamental difference between young and older people regarding *why* they go online, *how* they use dating platforms, and *what experiences* they have. By examining these age differences we can begin to understand the different ways in which people come to resort to online dating and to explain exactly why this new meeting venue has become so big.

Juvenile use: generational and age effects

The importance of online dating platforms for young people is partly due to a generational dynamic. Individuals born in and after the 1990s have grown up with new technology and been acclimatized to screens and digital culture from infancy. They use the internet more often, more intensively, and in more ways than the previous generations (Pew Research Center, 2018, 2019). This use is an integral part of their leisure activities, whether it comes in the form of listening to music, watching videos, films, or series, gaming, searching for information, or chatting with friends.

Dating platforms are part of this rich digital ecosystem. Interviews conducted with young users show that familiarity with social media makes online dating seem far less remarkable than it does to older adults. Downloading an app is not a major event, and using a platform is considered a banal experience. Usage is also less engaging and more periodic: young people connect from time to time, during lulls in their love lives or, more prosaically, when time allows, mainly in weekends and vacations. This is also evident from the big data from the Meetic Group platforms, which show that in July and August users aged 18–24 sign up more often than users from other age groups.[10] Younger generations have a distant, sometimes even phlegmatic relationship to online dating, which means that young people's threshold to signing up is low.

But this is only one part of the picture. The main reason why young people are the main users of dating platforms is not generational but related to age. On the one hand, singlehood is most common under the age of 30, and so it is in this age group that we find the largest numbers of people who are looking to meet partners. On the other hand, sexual exploration and falling in love are key features of youth experience and make online dating particularly appealing in youth. Among the youngest users, who are under the age of 25 and sometimes even in their teens, these platforms have become an important place for sexual and romantic socialization. Young people enjoy browsing through profiles, looking at photos, and chatting with people while these interactions do not necessarily move outside the online space; nor is that necessarily the aim. In 2019 in the United States, for instance, 30% of online dating users aged 18 to 29 declared that they had never gone on a date with anyone they met through an app or a site – by comparison to only 18% of those aged 30 to 49.[11] Undoubtedly the Covid-19 crisis and the concurrent lockdowns, which made it difficult or even impossible to meet face to face, have reinforced this trend but did not invent it. Online flirting has always been appreciated for its own sake. Dating apps are not only venues for meeting partners; they also serve as platforms for sexual sociability.

Online dating is sometimes performed collectively, especially by young women, when several log on at the same time, look at profiles together, and converse with often older men. The flirting is for fun, but it is also a way of gaining experience in intimate interactions. Many young women who were interviewed for this research talked about using dating platforms as a way of socializing among female friends:

> Sometimes we do it for fun; it's good for a laugh. There was one time, we were at my friend Mélanie's place and she told us about another app, it's called Fruitz, and she said: "Yes, I'm going to pick me some; it's been too long since I had something going on." And I said: "I'll download Tinder again." [...] And we went swiping through the profiles; it was great fun. (Camille, 22, student; parents: business owners)

The possibility of engaging in conversation from a safe distance, anonymously, and without anyone watching, allows for flirting more easily, without exposing oneself completely or feeling obliged to pursue contact. This feature is particularly appreciated by young women, for whom online flirtation is a way to test one's appeal and seek validation as a woman and as a partner. Being "liked" is reassuring and confirms that one conforms to gendered and heteronormative expectations. Dating apps lend themselves to this exercise by allowing women not only *to join* in the flirting game but also, and more importantly, *to leave* whenever they choose. Physical distance and the ability to end the conversation unilaterally at any time give women greater control in online interactions than in physical encounters, if men become disrespectful or aggressive. The countless stories women have shared as part of the #MeToo movement give enough evidence that men do not always accept that no means no. While dating sites and apps are not exempt from harassment and abusive behaviors (more on this in chapter 7), they make it possible to put the offender at a distance and to cease all contact. In this way, online dating allows young women to accomplish the female balancing act of seeking sexual validation without feeling compelled to take things further.

The experience is entirely different for young men, who are often encouraged to take an active role in romantic and sexual interactions. Theirs is a more "technical" approach to online flirting. If women seek confirmation of their attractiveness, considered as a personal trait, for men flirting is more of a skill to be learned and mastered, something that requires practice (Gourarier, 2013).

The Keys to Success 67

GREGORY: We really have very different roles. It's really up to the man to approach the woman. It's not really fair. I mean, that's how I see it. But that's just how it is!

INTERVIEWER: And did you approach anyone [on a dating site]?

GREGORY: I tried to. But since I never had done it, I didn't know how to. And that's the thing, I tried to learn about these things, you know. (Gregory, 23, student; mother: cleaner; father: construction worker)

Some young men invest dating platforms with the attributes of a training rink, where they can learn and practice the skills of dating and flirting. Young men are also much more eager to move from online conversation to in-person meeting. As Erving Goffman points out in his analysis of courtship, an "initial show of interest will often do" to confirm women in their heterosexual desirability, whereas actual physical access to a female provides a man with "evidence of his capacity as a male" (Goffman, 1977, p. 309). Thus, "whether the male is interested in courtship or mere seduction, he must pursue the female with intentions and she has the power to lengthen or shorten the pursuit" (pp. 309–310). These gendered codes may seem old-fashioned, even archaic, but they have not vanished. Online dating is a way for young people to see how well they measure up to conventional female and male norms. Rather than offering an escape from the gendered roles of courting and being courted, pursuing and being pursued, the platforms are often used to test one's ability to perform and endorse these very roles.

A hookup culture?

Online dating becomes more physical with age. While it is extremely rare for teenagers to take these interactions outside the online space, let alone have sex with someone encountered online, such actions become gradually more common among young adults. A Dutch survey conducted in 2017 showed that less than 2% of adolescents aged 12 to 17 had met in person with someone they knew from a dating app, and 0.5% had had sex with a person they met this way. Among 18–24-year-olds, around 14% had had a date via

68 The New Laws of Love

online dating, and 8% had had sex with a partner they met this way (De Graaf et al., 2018). These figures are consistent with the finds of a French survey conducted around the same time and showing that the proportion of young people who declared to have met a sexual partner online rose steadily from 3% among 15–17-year-olds to 8% among 18–19-year-olds, to 20% among 20–24-year-olds, and to 27% among 25–30-year-olds, before dropping progressively after the age of 30.[12]

Meeting sex partners online is hence common, primarily among young adults. This is how dating platforms have come to be associated with a "hookup culture" supposed to foster short-term sexual relationships at the expense of love and marriage. The debate on hookup culture is primarily North American, but the behaviors it refers to can be observed in most western countries. Over the past decades, it has become increasingly common to have several sexual partners during early adulthood. Young people experience a period of "sexual exploration" before settling down (Manning et al., 2005; Bajos and Bozon, 2012; Lyons et al., 2013). At the same time, relationships have also become much more fluid and diverse, ranging from "couples" to forms such as "friends with benefits," "fuck buddies," "hookups," or "regular hookups" – each language having its own words for new ways of being intimate (England et al., 2008).

This accumulation of experience has become the norm. Since formal education lasts longer and financial independence is delayed, greater value is placed on discovery and experimentation, in keeping with the idea that young adults should make the most of this part of their life. This norm is particularly strong among students, whose lifestyle and resources are conducive to the "exploration" ideal (Hamilton and Armstrong, 2009; Giraud, 2017), but is also present in less privileged environments. Working-class children, who typically leave formal education, start working, and enter adulthood at an earlier age, nonetheless share the same ideal of "making the most of it," which translates into an imperative to "have fun" (Clair, 2008). But this is not just a matter of amusement, it is also about learning. The desire is to gain experience, to learn to "know oneself," and to better know "what one wants." This is why some young people, students in particular, avoid entering into a long-term relationship "too early."

> I'm 22, and he and I have been going out together since I was 20. This may be somewhat naive, but I'm afraid that at 29 I'll look back and say "shit, I've been going out with him since I was 20." I was his first girlfriend, so I'd like him to see something else, so he can tell me whether or not I'm indeed the right woman, because when you have nothing to compare against, I don't know how you can tell if it's the right person or not. (Lucie, 22, student; mother: housewife; father: farmer)

This desire to accumulate experience is not, as we are sometimes led to believe, the sign of a general incapability to settle down. Alarmed writings on the hookup culture present youth sexuality as a "cultural shift" where "relationships have been replaced by the casual sexual encounters," as Laura Sessions Stepp (2007, p. 5) claims. There is no evidence for this claim from an empirical point of view. First, young people have both long-term and short-term partners. As Paula England and colleagues show from their large-scale survey on US students, the hookup has not killed the date, nor has it replaced romantic relationships, but young adults engage both in "couples" and in "casual sex" (England et al., 2008; Armstrong et al., 2010). In other words, there is no sign of substitution of one form of relationship (couples) with another (hookups), but rather a broadening of the relational repertoire.

Second, a large majority of women and men settle down when they become older (Manning et al., 2014). Getting married and having kids continues to be a life project for most young people, both men and women, and the tenacity of the couple norm stays remarkably strong in the western world (Roseneil et al., 2020). Early adulthood is seen as a time of provisional freedom, which young people recognize as fleeting, an opportunity to be seized before the fast approaching imperative to settle down and become a grown-up. This means that hookups do not represent a *culture* as much as a *life stage*. It is an experience bound to end; one must therefore try to capture it before it is too late.

70   The New Laws of Love

Online dating is particularly favored by – and in turn favors – this type of sexual exploration. It brings together numerous young people who are single and open to new experiences, but at the same time it is dissociated from ordinary social networks, and this makes it much more discreet. The possibility of interacting with a high guarantee of privacy is a salient feature. Indeed, sex and love are central to youth, but at this age intimate relationships are also subject to strong control exerted by family and friends. On dating platforms young people have the opportunity to flirt without anyone watching and to converse with and meet people new to them, whom they may not have dared to approach in other circumstances and whom they don't have to see again if they don't want to.

This is what makes online dating so popular. The possibility of going beyond one's immediate social circle is the most valuable aspect of what dating apps and sites offer. This also explains why Facebook, Snapchat, and other social networks are rarely seen as appropriate for dating, especially for casual dating. As another interviewee pointed out, "these are people you normally [already] know" (Bertrand, 22, student). Sharing friends and acquaintances with potential partners has become an important criterion, if not an absolute condition, when deciding whether to go intimate with someone, especially if the relationship is primarily sexual – in which case distance and anonymity are crucial. On many dating apps it is possible to see connections between users as the platforms have access to information from Facebook. Lucie, like many other interviewees, says she will systematically avoid people if there have any friends in common:

> There are people I could have matched with in normal circumstances, but when I saw we had so many mutual acquaintances, I said no. Yes, that's a deterrent; it immediately deters me, because I know that whatever happens between us might not stay between us. And even at the relationship level, I don't know if it's healthy to have so many friends in common. (Lucie, 22, student; mother: housewife; father: farmer)

To maintain social distance from potential partners is possible thanks to dating platforms and their inherent privatization of dating. This new possibility has recently turned into a principle. The disembeddedness of online dating with respect to ordinary social relations is not only a *matter of fact*; it has now become a *norm*. It is no longer considered "healthy," as Lucie says, to have the same friends as one's sexual partner. The diffusion of online dating is progressively cementing the idea that flirting and dating (especially when casual) ought to be distinct from other social spheres (work, education, social life, etc.) and that sexual and social networks are two different things. This aspect of online dating applies to all age groups, but has a different meaning for older users.

Tense thirties

The approach of the thirties brings the provisional freedom of youth to an end; plans develop to found a more stable relationship; and suggestions from family and friends to finally settle down grow more insistent (Bergström et al., 2019). Online dating now more often becomes an instrument in a quest to (re)partner, that is, to establish a lasting couple. In the opening line of her book *Future Sex*, Emily Witt pinpoints with humor this specific moment in life when the stakes change:

> I was single, straight, and female. When I turned thirty, in 2011, I still envisioned my sexual experience eventually reaching a terminus, like a monorail gliding to a stop at Epcot Center. I would disembark, find myself face-to-face with another human being, and there we would remain in our permanent station in life: the future. (Witt, 2016, p. 3)

Bit by bit, the exploration paradigm that characterizes youth gradually gives way to a more couple-oriented model associated with adulthood. In their late twenties, young people gradually establish couple relationships, move in together, and start to contemplate having a family. The propensity to form a couple accelerates on the threshold of the thirties, which is a turning point for many. The proportion of people living in a couple peaks around the

72 The New Laws of Love

age of 30 in many countries; in France for instance four in five people aged 30 to 34 report that they are in a stable relationship (Bergström et al., 2019).

This rise in the couple norm translates into an equal and opposite decline in the appeal of being single. A research project on singlehood conducted jointly with my colleagues Françoise Courtel and Géraldine Vivier showed that singles aged 30 to 34 are least satisfied with their situation. By comparison to other age groups, they are the least likely to say that singlehood is a deliberate choice and the most likely to report feeling excluded because they are not in a couple (Bergström et al., 2019). At this transitional age, being single is not only being in the minority; it is also being *marginalized*. For those on the wrong side of the divide, the desire to be in a relationship becomes more urgent and the couple norm can be oppressive. Questions from family and friends about a potential partner are a constant reminder that coupledom is the norm. This is also the time in life when women and men are most likely to seek potential partners, whether through online dating, by going to bars or clubs, or by asking people around them to introduce them to friends (Bergström et al., 2019).

The transition from the exploration paradigm to the couple model is not necessarily easy, nor is it free from tensions or disputes. Around the age of 30, misunderstandings between the sexes are commonplace and insults can fly. Women call men "bastards" on account of their unwillingness to commit to a "serious" relationship, while men accuse women of being "complicated," or even "uptight," because they demand clarity about the relationship's status before it has even started. In other words women of this age often desire to be in a committed relationship, while men want to keep their options open or prefer casual sex. This disagreement between the sexes was examined in a 2015 article in *Vanity Fair* titled "Tinder and the dawn of the 'Dating Apocalypse,'" which resonated internationally.[13] The title is taken from an interview with a 29-year-old female Tinder user who deplores the disruption of sexual norms and gender relations. The journalist discusses the so-called hookup culture and claims that it tips the balance heavily in favor of men. The idea is that, while women seek stable relationships, men turn to

The Keys to Success 73

serial encounters and ignore women's desire for commitment. Dating apps thus stand accused of making sex too easy and, more importantly, of serving men's interests.

The theoretical foundation of this common discourse is provided by Eva Illouz in *Why Love Hurts*. Taking a highly critical look at online dating, the author sees a "free market of sexual encounters" (Illouz, 2012, p. 10) that has given rise to a "new form of *emotional domination* of women by men, expressed in women's emotional availability and men's reluctance to commit to women, because the conditions of choice have changed" (p. 104). The basic idea is that, because men are more inclined than women to have sexual affairs, the casual nature of online dating works to men's advantage. Women, in the hope of finding love, accept sexual relations against their will, and thus emerge from the boom in online dating as its big losers.

This idea of gendered tensions around intimate relationships is not entirely false but picks up a specific moment in the life course. Although women have a more relational approach to sex than men (Hamilton and Armstrong, 2009), the conflict over the casual or serious status of the relationship is most acute at the ages that mark the transition from experimentation to couple life. Women begin this transition at an earlier age than men do. In France, for example, in the cohort born between 1977 and 1983, 90% of women, but only 75% of men, had lived with a partner before turning 30.[14] Data from the United States show consistent results: in 2019, 85% of women aged between 18 and 29 had already been in a committed romantic relationship, by comparison with 76% of the men the same age.[15] In other words, there is a delay between female and male trajectories, as men settle down later than women do. This means that men do not actually refuse to commit, only they do so at older ages.

Around the age of 30, this gap becomes obvious, and so does the difference between women's and men's desires. While some men still feel "young" and wish to take advantage of it, women of the same age start feeling "old" and are often impatient to form a couple and catch up with their female peers. This tension is far less pronounced at younger ages, when many young women want to experiment and "have fun" just as young men do (as we have seen). It relaxes

74   The New Laws of Love

again at older ages, when both sexes place great value on committed relationships, as I will discuss in the next section. By the age of 40, men actually live in a couple more often than women, and after a separation they couple up more often and more quickly than women do (Wu and Schimmele, 2005; Beaujouan, 2012; Di Nallo, 2019). The conflict over commitment is less of a "war between the sexes" than is sometimes claimed in the hookup literature (Bogle, 2008); it is rather a gendered difference in the timing of the transition between two life stages. The provisional freedom of youth is shorter for women than for men.

The thirties thus appear as a critical moment in the life course, one in which women and men progressively transition from one model to another. At older ages, the stakes change again. Among separated, divorced, and widowed individuals, the desire to repartner is often strong among both women and men, but in midlife the opportunities to do so are significantly reduced.

Back in the game: midlife dating

Most women and men experience living in a couple at least once in their lives, and those who separate often form a new union quickly afterward. In France, in 2013, half of the people aged 26 to 65 who had separated were back living in a couple within two years (INSEE, 2015). The ambition to start afresh and to fall in love again is often supported by the environment. Interviews with older and separated individuals, typically over 30, show that friends and family strongly encourage them to sign up to a dating platform and sometimes even take charge of it themselves.

> When they found out that I was no longer with – I can say "my companion" because he was more of a friend at the end [laughs], he was more like a life companion – all my female friends said, "Go find someone [...] you mustn't stay on your own." And one of my friends told me, "Go look on the internet! [...] I have lots of female friends who do it; it's great." So, she suggested a website; I looked at it, and I signed up. (Véronique, 68, retired head of advertising agency, no children)

The Keys to Success 75

You can always find love, and you should always try to: that's the message, and sometimes the pressure, that comes from family and friends. But forming a couple requires meeting a partner. Instead of passively waiting, women and men are encouraged to take control of their lives, notably by signing up to a dating platform. This ethic of self-responsibility is present in many social spheres, and particularly in one's work life. At a time of increasingly discontinuous life trajectories – whether in employment, in residency, or in relationships – individuals are expected more than ever to take charge of their destiny (Van de Velde, 2011). In matters of the heart, taking charge translates into a proactive approach to meeting new people. Once again, the seasonality of registrations for online dating services is highly revealing. Data from the Meetic Group platforms show that, while young people join mainly in the summer, during vacation, older users sign up more often in January, that is, in a month that symbolizes a fresh start.[16]

As the couple norm becomes stronger and more demanding, the opportunities to meet partners diminish. This situation is familiar to singles who see the field of possibilities narrow with age. Interviewees older than 30 years stress that their social life offers few possibilities to meet new people and deplore the absence of singles among their acquaintances:

> When you get older, the people around you are married with children, and you can't go out anymore. I personally don't have any friends who are single; the people around me are all married couples. So, for starters, I can't go out with a girlfriend who's single, let's say, go to a restaurant on a Saturday night, or on weekends when I don't have the kids; I can't do that, because they're all in couples. And when my friends invite me over, it's always at their place, with the same people, the same couples; it's impossible to meet anyone new. It's a vicious circle. (Patricia, 38, registered nurse, two young children)

Singlehood is common in youth and potential partners are then plenty, but later on the situation changes. After the age of 30, those who have not yet settled down or have separated have precious few opportunities for (re)partnering. On the one hand, most friends (and friends of friends) are already in

76 The New Laws of Love

a relationship, as Patricia observed. On the other hand, many dating contexts used by younger people are no longer accessible or are considered "inappropriate" for someone older.

> SYLVIE: Today, if you want to meet someone, there aren't all that many solutions, especially in my age group.
> INTERVIEWER: What's changed?
> SYLVIE: When you're younger, you can go to bars, you know. In bars, you can meet people. But at my age I can't go to bars, it wouldn't be appropriate now. So, there's no way of meeting people spontaneously anymore. (Sylvie, 57, economically inactive, two adult children)

Sylvie met her former husband in a bar, when she was 23; today, at 57, she rules out the possibility of meeting someone in a similar setting. Cafés, clubs, and other festive venues are widely frequented by young people but deemed inappropriate "after a certain age." Twenty-eight-year-old Élodie reports that she has "left behind my crazy days when I was always going out to clubs with friends" and has now transitioned to "quiet evenings with my friends." Indeed, the end of youth coincides with a transformation of social life. There are fewer outings to public places (bars, clubs, shows, or other public events) and there is more socializing indoors, whether at dinners and parties at home or in other private settings (e.g. going out to restaurants with friends; Forsé, 1999; Litwin and Stoeckel, 2013). At the same time, social networks contract into smaller circles as socializing with friends tends to give way to socialization with the family (Marsden and Srivastava, 2012; Rainie and Wellman, 2012). This affects not only people who have entered family life as couples but also their single friends, who have now fewer people to go out with. "People who are in a relationship, on the weekends, they're happy to be together. I'm not gonna be the single girlfriend who bugs everyone, going 'Hey there, I'm bored at my place.' [Laughs]" (Patricia, 38).

This contraction of the dating landscape makes online dating an increasingly important meeting venue (McWilliams and Barrett, 2014; Dwyer et al., 2020). Many older users, who are not brought up on internet, are reluctant or even hostile at first, but after a breakup or an extended period of singlehood their attitude to dating platforms changes. This can be seen even among those who are least comfortable with the prospect.

> I'd been hearing about those sites for a while and I thought, no, never, I just don't see the point. And then after some time, given that I was alone, and it's not always easy to meet new people when you've tried all your friends, or even to go to parties... and then you see there's nothing that could lead to something concrete. So you say to yourself: I'll just join a dating site [smile]. That's how it happened, with Meetic. But at first, it wasn't a natural step for me. (Bruno, 44, welder, two teenage children)

It is, once more, the possibility to go beyond one's immediate environment to meet new people that explains the popularity of online dating. While young people enjoy the discretion it offers, older users are attracted by the promise of broadening the pool of potential partners. The rising rates of separation stand in sharp contrast with the scarcity of meeting venues for middle-aged individuals. Social life is often restricted during this period of life as a result of work, the presence of children, and age-specific norms about appropriate leisure activities for "mature" women and men. This is why couples formed through online dating are primarily older (Rosenfeld and Thomas, 2012; Bergström, 2016b). Youth culture and student life afford ample opportunities to make new acquaintances, and so online dating is a supplement rather than a substitute. Later on the situation changes radically and, as social life contracts, online dating comes to play a greater part.

The higher success rate for older people, measured in couple formation, can also be explained by the fact that people in this age group may show determination (Danielsbacka et al., 2020). Unlike younger adults, they seldom use online dating routinely, as a matter of course; rather they act on a deliberate decision to seek a new life partner, a decision that involves "giving yourself a good kick in the butt" (Delphine, 32, social worker), or even "forcing yourself" to go ahead with it (Patricia, 38, nurse). When the age for discovery and exploration is over, the objective is not "having fun" as much as "taking charge of things."

* * *

78 The New Laws of Love

Online dating is not a universal experience. It differs according to many factors such as age, gender, social class, sexual orientation, and geographic location, as well as according to psychological variables such as mental health and well-being. I have just started to unwrap the diversity of usage by insisting on age, which I believe to be one of the most central variables for understanding the contrasting motives and experiences associated with online dating. Indeed, these platforms are used in very different ways by adolescents, younger adults, singles in their thirties, and older separated people. I have not mentioned here senior usage, which comes with yet different stakes, but will get to it in chapter 6. What is obvious from online dating is that there are distinct "chapters" in life, in the form of different periods associated with sexual and emotional experiences. Online dating both benefits from this evolution and actively participates in it.

This forces us to revisit the matter of how we account for the success of online dating. We are accustomed to conceive of this new phenomenon as a result of new norms. Hedonist and consumerist values are often advanced in explanation of young people's sexual use of dating apps, whereas rationalism is commonly thought to drive separated people to use these platforms. This reading is based on a profoundly *ideational* viewpoint, according to which norms, values, and ideology are the driving forces of history that cause changes in behavior. The study of online dating leads me to adopt the opposite perspective and to reverse the direction of causality: new norms also arise from changes in practice.

Indeed, online dating owes a lot to structural changes in life conditions. First, its use by young adults – a use that is often decried as the embodiment of a new hookup culture spurred by changing sexual norms – finds its origin in the economic and social conditions of contemporary youth. Adulthood has been delayed, hence youth is associated with uncertainty, exploration, and a gradual path to independence. The transient nature of young people's relationships must be understood in this specific context, of a period of life when things are on hold. Longer school enrolment has not only allowed for this provisional freedom but also provided norms of discovery, learning, and self-development that are transferred into the intimate sphere. In other words, the reason

The Keys to Success 79

why young people resort to online dating and what they do on these platforms have everything to do with the economic and social situation associated with youth.

Similarly, when older adults turn to online dating in order to seek a partner, they are not merely conforming to new norms. More than anything else, they are struggling against the odds of meeting a new partner, given that, for both social and demographic reasons, dating conditions deteriorate as the years go by. For sure, women and men who sign up to dating platforms often do so with a pragmatic approach and with an ethic of self-responsibility. But these attitudes do not arise out of nothing; they are firmly rooted in contemporary life conditions. Professional, residential, and relational trajectories have become complex and discontinued, and lead women and men to adopt both a realistic and a voluntaristic approach to life. Online dating cannot be fully understood if we look only to *ideational* variables, without taking into account these *material* factors that have profoundly changed intimacy.

4

Time for Sex and Love

Online dating is routinely accused of killing love, not only because of the "unromantic" mechanics of swiping profiles but, more importantly, because the resulting relationships are assumed to be more about sex than about romance. Reports focus on casual sex and the lack of commitment, and the high turnover of online partners is denounced as the sign of looser morals or of a consumerist approach to intimacy. Whatever the case, there has been talk of a sexual revolution 2.0 and of the diffusion of new attitudes towards sex – attitudes that are more playful, more narcissistic, more utilitarian, or more liberated, depending on which voices we listen to. The argument runs that this new sexual culture is nurtured by online dating and, more generally, by the disinhibition that characterizes online interactions.

What can surveys tell us? Online dating has undeniably changed sexual behavior: the relationships formed online become sexual more rapidly and are often short-lived. However, the explanation lies less in the emergence of new attitudes to sexuality than in a profound change of *context*. The reason why online dating differs from "ordinary" dating is, first and foremost, that the material conditions for inter-action and for relationship formation are not the same. Online dating occurs *outside* one's social circles, and often *out of sight*. This discretion marks a departure from the openness

Time for Sex and Love

of ordinary situations (e.g. work, school, parties and outings) insofar as it considerably alleviates the external control of sexuality. By making dating private, these platforms facilitate casual relationships and profoundly modify the heterosexual scripts.

A sexual revolution or recession?

In discussions on change in sexual behavior and norms, the 1960s and 1970s often serve as a reference point, as these decades mark what has been labeled a "sexual revolution." The expression refers to a series of developments in family and intimate life such as the decline of marriage, the rise of premarital sex, the growing visibility and acceptance of same-sex relationships, and the increasing number of sexual partners (Hekma and Giami, 2014). The generations born in the 1940s or later entered adulthood on different terms by comparison to older cohorts.

This was not much of a revolution, though. In fact many changes in sexual conduct that occurred in the latter part of the twentieth century came about progressively. Age at first intercourse, for instance, has gradually dropped over the decades in the western world, but there is no specific breaking point (Mercer et al., 2013; Bajos et al., 2018). The increase in cohabitations, divorce rates, and births out of wedlock follows a similar trend: the rise more often follows a smooth curve than a sharp shift (González-Val and Marcén, 2012; Klüsener, 2015; Kok and Leinarte, 2015).

The common idea that norms have loosened and given way to a sexual "liberation" can also be questioned. Values and beliefs around sex have changed, to be sure, and some relationships that were considered morally unacceptable in mid-twentieth century (e.g. unmarried couples or homosexual relationships) are now "normal." However, old norms have been replaced by new ones: sexual emancipation, gender equality, and sexual consent form a new moral system. And, while some types of sexual relations have been decriminalized (e.g. same-sex relations), others are more heavily penalized than ever (e.g. non-consensual sex and pedophilia). Rather than a turning point in the 1960s and

82   The New Laws of Love

1970s, we observe a set of profound and long-lasting trans-formations over several decades and a progressive normative turn toward ideals of self-fulfillment and mutual respect (Bozon, 2004).

The internet has not altered this. Nor has there been a digital revolution in sexual behavior in the last decades any more than a sexual revolution in the 1960s and 1970s. This, too, goes against common belief. New technology in general and online dating in particular are said to have had a major impact on sexuality. The most widespread perception is that sexual behavior has been unleashed; the hookup debate illustrates this idea very well. More recently, however, the wind has turned: rather than too much sex, the internet now stands accused of creating too little of it. In 2018 the journalist Kate Julian stated that, "despite the easing of taboos and the rise of hookup apps, Americans are in the midst of a sex recession."[1] The article, published in *The Atlantic*, gained much attention both in North America and in Europe, where several magazines published reportages on the same theme, raising the alarm that young people were having less sex than in previous generations. Glued to their mobile phones and hooked on Netflix, internet porn, or dating apps, the generations born in and after the 1990s are supposedly incapable of and uninterested in creating physical connections in real life (Twenge, 2017). Whereas parents traditionally worried about their children having sex too early, they now seem bothered about their having sex too late. Whatever they do, the kids are never all right...

To what extent has sexual behavior changed because of the internet and, more specifically, because of online dating? There are three empirical ways of answering this question. In order to determine whether people are having more sex or less sex, we can look at the age of sexual debut, the number of partners over the life course, and the frequency of sexual intercourse.

Regarding the first indicator, age at first intercourse tends to be stable or declining in Europe since the year 2000, as shown by data from the United Kingdom, France, and the Scandinavian countries (Mercer et al., 2013; Bajos et al., 2018; Hansen et al., 2020). The United States and the Netherlands are exceptions: the youngest generations, born in 1990s and later, report having had sex at a later age than older generations (Finer and Philbin, 2014; de Graaf et al., 2017). But in most of these countries, whether the age is declining or increasing, changes are small, and by the age of 30 a large majority of women and men are sexually active. This makes it difficult to talk of a "sexual counter-revolution"[2] or a generation "no sex."[3]

The number of sexual partners over the life course tends to follow a progressive increase from the 1990s onward; this is the case in the United Kingdom, France, and the United States. In these countries the increase is significant for women, whereas for men the trend is more stable (Mercer et al., 2013; Bajos et al., 2018). However, sexual activity itself, the third indicator, is reported to decline in several countries. The number of times individuals had sexual intercourse in the last year (per week, per month or per year), has gone down in the United States in the recent period and more generally since 2000 (Twenge et al., 2017; Ueda et al., 2020). Similar results were found in other countries, for instance Finland (Kontula, 2015).

This trend has one major explanation, which is unrelated to new technology: the increasing number of single people. Individuals in a stable relationship are more likely to have regular sex than individuals who are unpartnered, which means that, when singlehood goes up, as it has over the last decades, sexual activity mechanically drops. This being said, another pattern is a decrease in sexual activity among partnered and married individuals. This might be due to many things, for example a more stressful lifestyle, changing norms, or new behaviors such as digital practice; we can only hypothesize on the matter. What appears clear, however, is that that online dating has little to do with a presumed "sex recession."

The most notable change in sexuality brought about by online dating lies elsewhere: it can be found in the *timing* of interactions. Relationships that begin on dating platforms follow a sequence of events of their own and advance at a different pace; they quickly become sexual, and they are often short-lived.

The acceleration of dating

Online dating makes everything go faster. That's what users say, and that's what surveys show, too. When two people appreciate each other, they often decide quickly to meet in person, and if the first impressions pass this test the relationship soon becomes sexual. This scenario holds for all kinds of dating; but, in the absence of survey data on casual affairs, I will start by focusing on couple relationships.

The French EPIC survey on couple formation measured the number of days between initial contact and first sexual intercourse and allows us to compare timings of events according to where and how couples first meet (see Figure 4.1). Results show that relationships formed on online dating platforms become sexual faster than other relationships. In more than a half of the couples (56%) that met this way, the partners had known each other for no longer than a month when they first had sex together. In almost a third (31%), they had known each other for no more than a week. This is a very short time by comparison to what happens in other relationships. For people who met at a party with friends, for example, several months often elapse before there is sex. The time is even longer for people who meet at work: only 8% of

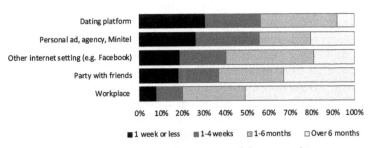

Figure 4.1. Time between initial contact and first sexual intercourse among couples in France (%)

Scope: Romantic relationships formed in France by individuals aged 26–65, in five different contexts, from 2005 to 2013 (for dating platform, other internet setting, party with friends, and workplace) or from 1970 to 2013 (for personal ads, marriage agencies, and Minitel).

Source: EPIC survey (France, 2013–14, INED–INSEE).

Time for Sex and Love

the relationships formed in this setting become sexual within a week – in most cases the interval is several months. Online dating shortens the courtship phase between first contact and first intercourse.

The explanation lies mainly in the unequivocal nature of dating platforms by comparison to other situations. Things are more ambiguous at a party with friends, for instance, where there may be no clear distinction between being friendly and flirting. What is more, people may not know whether the other person is free. In a situation of uncertainty, it takes time to check that desires and intentions are reciprocated and to develop a closer bond. This is the case even more when future partners meet at work, as Virginie remarks:

> You can't do the same things in the workplace as you would do somewhere else. So we took the time to get to know each other over the course of a month, because we both set limits for ourselves. We used that month to get to know each other differently from if we had simply met at a party. There was mutual flirting, yes, but it was subtle. (Virginie, 29, social worker)

Romantic and sexual relationships that begin in the workplace are sensitive, not only because employers and colleagues may disapprove, but because they require a great deal of work to redefine the relationship. As Virginie puts it, this involves getting to know each other "differently." Transitioning from a work situation to a potentially sexual situation takes time and involves a series of rituals. The partners must translate the professional relation into a "sexual script" – to use a term coined by John H. Gagnon and William Simon (2005) – in order for both of them to recognize the situation as sexual. This process is often long, but it allows the two protagonists to test the waters, carefully calibrate their expectations, and gradually come closer. This preliminary phase is much shorter in the context of online dating, as users of all ages pointed out in the interviews.

> It's the difference between real life and Tinder. I mean, generally, in real life, with a girl you meet in your social

circle, you'll wait, you'll both take your time, it'll begin with a cigarette and gradually you'll start talking, and you'll go on talking, you add each other on Facebook and then, two weeks later, you might decide to go for it. On Tinder there is a different paradigm, a different dimension, as things go faster. (Corentin, 25; mother: communication manager; father: production manager)

There is such a difference between online and in-person dating that Corentin speaks of a "different paradigm." It is true that dating platforms frame interactions in a particular way. Signing up to such an app or site means stating publicly that one is single and open to a romantic or sexual relationship. Similarly, contacting someone (or responding) will be immediately understood as a sign of sexual interest. The ambiguity that often characterizes other social interactions is completely absent: the only reason for two people to communicate is to assess each other as potential partners.

This unambiguous framing of online dating is what accelerates the course of events. In a situation where people are clear about the intimate nature of their relationship, the risk of misreading the other person's cues and losing face is considerably reduced, and so the partners make their advance with greater certainty. As one user put it, with online dating "some things are given [...] there are prerequisites that really facilitate the relationship" (Luc, 48, publisher). Relationships thus quickly become physical (through touching and kissing) and sexual. The fact that sexual or romantic intentions are out in the open means that the "definition of the situation" is sexual from the outset (Thomas, 1923).

The phenomenon is specific to dating platforms and does not apply to the digital world in general. For instance, relationships that arise on social network platforms such as Facebook, Snapchat, Instagram, or Twitter follow a different scenario. The online conversation phase is longer, and it takes more time for the relationship to become sexual – often more than a month after the first contact, as the French survey shows (see Figure 4.1). These relationships resemble those that begin at a party much more than those formed on a dating platform. Because digital social networks are often closely linked to ordinary social circles

Time for Sex and Love 87

and because relationships on those networks are framed as friendly or professional rather than sexual, they progress through the same tentative back-and-forth as when people meet in person. Therefore relationships will build more gradually.

This makes it clear that what speeds things up is not the *digital nature* of online dating (or the presumed disinhibiting effect of the internet), but the fact that these platforms are *dating services*. For the same reason, personal ads, marriage agencies, and the Minitel messaging services – which are built around explicit motives, too – were similarly characterized by a rapid transition to sex (see Figure 4.1). The close resemblance, in terms of sexual scripts, between dating apps and these former matchmaking services means that sexual conduct on dating platforms is not due to *new attitudes* induced by the internet or late capitalism. It is all a matter of context.

No strings attached

Relationships that start off on dating platforms do not only become sexual very fast, they are also often short-lived. The widespread image of online dating as a realm of casual sex is indeed confirmed by statistical surveys. The French EPIC survey showed that, among the respondents aged 26 to 65 who had ever used a dating site, fewer than one in five (19%) reported having formed a couple or a serious relationship via a dating site. On the other hand, just over a half of them (51%) said that they had had less serious relationships, either romantic or sexual, by using these sites.[4] Dating platforms yield many dates, many of which become sexual, but only a minority of the resulting relationships are long-lasting.

This is consistent with the prevailing view. When asked about the image of dating sites, more than a half of the respondents to the French EPIC survey agreed to the proposition that they "lead mostly to casual encounters" (55%), and the percentage was even higher (70%) among those who had actually used an online dating site.[5] A more recent survey, from the Pew Research Institute in the United States, shows similar results, although the question was more vague.

88   The New Laws of Love

Respondents, all aged 18 or older, were asked whether "relationships where people first meet through a dating site or app are just as successful as those that begin in person." To this, 54% answered that online relationships were just as successful, 38% said that they were less successful, and only a marginal proportion, 5%, thought they were more successful than relationships that begin in person.[6] Both surveys indicate that online dating is strongly associated with a sexual scenario, both in terms of representations (what we think we know about online dating), and in terms of practice (the actual experience of it).

This image of online dating sometimes translates into a self-fulfilling prophecy: because people do not expect that online dating can be "serious" or lead to anything but casual sex, they end up with just that and don't hope for more (Bergström, 2011a). This explains in part the transient nature of many online relationships. Another contributing factor is the acceleration of dating. Since intercourse occurs early, many relationships become sexual before the partners have decided on their nature or future. The specific tempo of online dating makes short-term relationships a constitutive part of the user experience even when users do not necessarily want this feature.

But, most importantly, the inherent characteristics of online dating favor casual encounters. Users are more disposed to having non-committal sex, or entering relationships of an unclear status, with partners they meet on such platforms, because of the discretion that the latter allow. The fact that relationships begin and unfold without scrutiny gives one considerable autonomy in managing one's private life. This is less the case in ordinary social situations. For instance, Tanguy says he is wary of "gossip" at university: "You do something and two days later everyone knows all about it" (Tanguy, 22). Something similar happens in friendship groups, as Paul explains:

> Trying to pick someone up at a party can be complicated because the women are either friends or friends of friends. There's always trouble and it creates lots of problems, like: he went out with so-and-so, or someone doesn't like so-and-so going out with someone else, and there are ex-boyfriends,

Time for Sex and Love

and so on. It just makes things more complicated. It's easier to meet new people online, who are really new, who are outside all that, people you're not going to have those kinds of problems with. (Paul, 26, web marketing manager)

Many settings that offer the opportunity of meeting new people (university, work, parties, social events, and so on) have the drawback of providing an often unwanted audience. Dating someone in the same circle of friends, acquaintances or colleagues never goes unnoticed and often becomes a topic of curiosity, conversation, and sometimes criticism. People are expected to account for their actions to an entourage that feels entitled to know what is going on. Sharing the same social environment with someone also means having frequent contacts with that person. This is why Alix avoids going out or hooking up with students from her own university:

I'm not going to date a guy from my university because I don't want to see him every day if it doesn't work out. I don't want to see him with another girl if it doesn't work out. I just don't want any complications. That's why I really prefer it to be outside all that. (Alix, 21, student; mother: housewife; father: lawyer)

Online dating is less consequential than ordinary dating. As another user says, "It's less of a problem. [...] in any event, she's not a friend of a friend, and so, in any event, you don't care" (Sébastien, 29). Here again, it's not the digital nature of the platforms that matters; casual affairs are generally more common in situations that are disconnected from a person's regular everyday life. Vacation and holiday spots, for instance, are known to foster short-term relationships because they are frequented on a temporary basis and partners are unlikely to cross each other's path unless they wish to do so (Bozon and Rault, 2012). Dating apps and sites offer a similar setting. By disembedding dating from ordinary social life, they make it easier both to begin and to end intimate relationships.

This feature is particularly salient to certain groups, for instance the LGBT community, which uses online dating to a far greater extent than the heterosexual population (Rosenfeld and Thomas, 2012; Bergström, 2016b). Part of the explanation lies in the fact that users of gay or lesbian apps are, by definition, identified as bisexual or homosexual (whereas some "gaydar" may be needed in ordinary social circumstances), and the platforms are better screened from homophobia. Another factor is that dating platforms make it possible to distinguish between sexual practice and self-presentation. This is of course important in contexts where homosexuality carries a heavy stigma or is criminalized. Interestingly, it can also be valued in contexts where homosexuality is, on the contrary, widely accepted and comes to be assimilated along with heterosexual norms. In his work on gay online hookups, Kane Race points out that, "at a time when marriage and monogamy increasingly monopolize the public discourse of gay desire, the capacity to maintain a loose web of fuckbuddies is perhaps more available, more accessible, and more widely accessed than ever before" (Race, 2015, p. 271). Online dating is appealing because it allows for "a potential disconnect between people's normative identifications and their actual sexual practices" (p. 271).

The significance of separating one's social identity from one's sexual conduct is well established in the literature on same-sex relations. But it is rarely acknowledged that this possibility is also central to heterosexuals, especially women. The sexual double standard creates a situation where women are judged differently, typically more severely, than men when it comes to sexual conduct (Lamont, 2020). While in men casual relationships can be seen as something positive – proofs of manhood, for instance – in women they are thought to violate the norm of female sexual reserve. The tenacity of this double standard has been stressed by many scholars, both European and North-American, and is a key result of the research on hookups conducted by Paula England and colleagues: "women who hook up with too many people, or have casual sex readily, are called 'sluts' by both men and women" (England et al., 2008, p. 565; see also Fjær et al., 2015). Interviews with female users of online dating illustrate how women put their reputation on the line whenever they engage in sexual relations and how, consequently, they exercise caution in order to avoid moral disapproval:

As much as I fully assume my lifestyle during phases when I don't feel like having anything serious, I'm fully aware of the image it can convey to some people. I know full well it could very easily be considered slutty, or who knows what. So it's an image you want not to convey. (Virginie, 29, social worker)

Online dating has not eradicated this gendered sexual morality, but provides a means to shield from it temporarily. It offers platforms for engaging in sexual experimentation and in short-term relationships with less risk of stigma from one's entourage. Indeed, by keeping these experiences outside one's social circle and possibly unknown to it, one can both engage in morally contested sexual conduct and keep a respectable image of sexual modesty. For women, just as for any group of people who are potentially stigmatized for their sexuality, this contributes to the appeal of online dating. For the same reason these platforms facilitate access to sex, be it lesbian, gay, or straight.

The new shapes of love

So then, has online dating killed love? Many authors answer in the affirmative and adduce as proof the large number of online hookups, which they regard as an inherent threat to romantic long-term relationships. This viewpoint is shared by Laura Sessions Stepp, the author of *Unhooked: How Young Women Pursue Sex, Delay Love and Lose at Both*. As the title intimates, the author is particularly worried about hookups among young girls and urges them to "consider that having sex with lots of men might limit their ability to sustain a long-term commitment as well as their ability to conceive children" (Sessions Stepp, 2007, p. 7). The reasoning is that of a zero-sum game: the number of sexual relationships is supposed to correlate negatively with the probability of establishing a romantic one.

A similar argument comes from proponents of the choice overload theory. According to Renata Salecl (2010, p. 75), the hookup culture has given us a world in which "lack of commitment is the new vogue in relationships." She

92 The New Laws of Love

deplores particularly "the abundance of choice and the interchangeability that characterize internet dating" (p. 83). The argument is that, when supplied with a steady stream of potential partners and tempted by the hope of finding someone "better," people are incapable of settling for someone in particular, as they are always looking for something new. Eva Illouz's latest book *The End of Love* follows a similar line of reasoning; the new paradigm of choice is understood to be in direct antagonism with commitment. Once more, online dating platforms are treated as an important social force in this "unloving" trend (Illouz, 2019).

Yet, as the statistics presented in chapter 3 show, online dating platforms have become an important meeting venue for long-term couples as well. Whether these romantic relationships last less than other couples is not entirely clear. A German study found that individuals who met in any online setting broke up more frequently than individuals who met in other ways (Danielsbacka et al., 2020). Studies conducted in the United States tend to show either a lower breakup rate for online couples than for in-person relationships (Cacioppo et al., 2013), or no difference in longevity between couples formed on dating platforms and couples that met elsewhere (Rosenfeld, 2017). What seems clear, however, is that partners who know each other through online dating commit more easily than others. Different surveys from the United States, Germany, and Switzerland show that these online couples get married more rapidly than other couples do (Rosenfeld, 2017) and that they more frequently show intentions to have children (Danielsbacka et al., 2020; Potârcă, 2020). These empirical findings strongly contradict theories according to which online dating causes or favors loss of commitment.

Online dating does not challenge love and commitment themselves, but has changed the corresponding notions. This change is a growing dissociation between sex and coupledom. This is a historical movement and has its beginning in the mid-twentieth century. In his work on how sex is articulated onto couple formation, the French sociologist Michel Bozon showed that, while in the 1950s the first sexual intercourse coincided with marriage and came after a period of "chaste" courtship, the pattern was progressively reversed from the

Time for Sex and Love

1970s on: sexual relations started to be initiated early, well before cohabitation, and certainly before marriage. This change in the timing and sequencing of events reflects changes in the role of sex in romantic relationships. Previously considered a *consequence* of the union, sexual intimacy became a way of *establishing* the couple in the 1970s: "the first sexual intercourse [is] really the foundational act of the bond between two people" (Bozon, 1991b, pp. 69–70).

Online dating involves a further change in the role of sex, as the first intercourse occurs even earlier in the sequence. For partners who meet online, sex is a way of validating that there is a mutual interest, rather than the unique event signifying that they form a couple: sex merely signifies that coupledom is a possible horizon. This means that the partners become lovers before the nature of the relationship has been defined and before their mutual feelings have been clarified. This has two important implications.

First, relationships are not necessarily exclusive. Meeting someone online – which is seen as opening the field of possibilities rather than closing it – does not necessarily entail unsubscribing from dating platforms, or no longer seeing other people. This fact underlies complaints that online dating fuels a "commitment phobia" (Kaufmann, 2010; Illouz, 2012). This term, however, fails to account for what is new in the situation. The willingness to see other people is less a matter of indecisiveness than an expression of the fact that physical intimacy begins very early in the dating process, well before the partners consider themselves a couple. Exclusiveness is postponed until later, when the relationship is more fully established and the time comes to consider "where we stand relative to each other," as one woman stated in her interview (Françoise, 60). Rather than a fear of engaging in a romantic relationship, what we observe is a new path towards couple formation, in which the partners spend time together and have sex together before making a commitment.

Second, this means that entering a relationship is no longer marked by actions or events – say, the first kiss, or the first sexual intercourse – but by *words*. Only when the partners say to each other that they are indeed a couple – and present themselves as such to their environments – will they consider themselves as actually being a couple. In the past, things were different; many things simply went unsaid, as having sex meant being in a (presumably exclusive) relationship. Today, however, when online dating expands the possibility of meeting other partners, when sex occurs earlier, and in the absence of exclusiveness in the initial phases of relationships, couple formation is increasingly based on an explicit verbal commitment. As sexuality and conjugality are dissociated, couple formation becomes a speech act.

* * *

Online dating is not a new sexual revolution. It participates in a series of long-term evolutions and in extending them. The first of these evolutions is the increasing autonomy of sexuality vis-à-vis couple relationships. Not only does physical contact occur early on in relationships (often long before partners consider themselves as a couple), but the repertoire for heterosexual relationships has become much more diverse; it ranges from "couples" and "serious relationships" to "fuckbuddies," "hookups," and "friends with benefits." Lacking any institutional status, these relationships are framed by what Sharman Levinson calls "reference stories," that is, cultural scripts that make it possible to name and differentiate between the relations according to the meeting venue, the type of partner, the timing, and the course of events (Levinson, 2001). Online dating participates in this diversification of intimate relationships.

It also contributes to a change in the control of sexuality. The influence exerted by traditional authorities (e.g. the family and organized religion) may have waned since the middle of the twentieth century, but the space has since been occupied. The vertical control of sexuality has been replaced by a horizontal one, exerted by peers and, notably, by friends. At the same time, competing moral messages with a more diffuse influence are voiced in the media, but also through education and science: rather than outright prohibitions, they present models of self-accomplishment that call upon individual responsibility (Bozon, 2004). Online dating accentuates these tendencies. Dissociated from ordinary social life, it allows for sexual relationships not only beyond the family's ken, but also outside the knowledge of one's peers. The social networks (friends, colleagues, acquaintances) that

Time for Sex and Love

traditionally play an important role in romantic and sexual encounters are now deprived of their control over emerging relationships.

However radical these changes may appear, they do not signal sexual emancipation. The modes by which sexuality is regulated have changed, but they have not disappeared. As external control has lessened, internalized controls have grown in their place: greater sexual leeway has brought new demands, men and women being expected more than ever before to use their freedom wisely and responsibly. This results in self-examination. Many online dating users continuously question whether their conduct is appropriate and consistent with their personal ideals and values. Self-scrutiny, auto-correction, and self-censorship are common among both men and women; examples are fixing a maximum number of dates per week or month, deciding not to have sex on a first date (a decision common among women), doing "detox" by temporarily suspending usage, or even quitting online dating altogether. These self-regulating practices, which aim at a sexually healthy and responsible usage, full of respect for oneself and others, are the new sexual morality. Faced with a seemingly unlimited access to sex, each individual is summoned to define for herself or himself a proper sexual conduct. Online dating has made self-governance the primary mode of control of contemporary sexuality.

Part 2
Unequal before the Laws of Love

5

Class at First Sight

In his book *Distinction*, Pierre Bourdieu demonstrated how the social barriers that pervade society come into play in judgments about what counts as valuable and beautiful. Class distinctions are inherent in matters of taste – in one's liking and disliking what others may prize in such areas as music, film, literature, and food. These distinctions are far from innocent, as they contribute to perpetuating social stratification and, ultimately, the domination of the upper classes (Bourdieu, 1984). Bourdieu argued that the same forces are at work in matters of the heart: birds of a feather flock together, and hence they consolidate social class.

Is it still so? Critics claim that this 1970s portrayal of a class-based society is largely outdated. Indeed, western countries have undergone considerable change in the subsequent four decades, starting with a shift from manufacturing to a services-oriented economy. The expansion of formal education has opened up high schools and universities to children from working-class backgrounds and, perhaps more importantly, has encouraged more fluid interactions between youth cultures. What is more, the growth of a mass culture means that, today more than ever before, we share a common cultural ground. This has been interpreted as an attenuation of social stratification, and even as the death of class (Pakulski and Waters, 1996).

100   The New Laws of Love

Online dating platforms seem to exemplify this blurring of social boundaries. As general mass-market services, they are highly popular in all strata of society, and many platforms have a socially diverse user base, with people from various backgrounds. Nevertheless, social stratification is strong in the digital world. In his book *The Structure of Digital Partner Choice*, the German sociologist Andreas Schmitz shows not only how partner preferences, choices, and strategies are profoundly marked by class, but also how relevant a Bourdieusian perspective on online dating can be. Interactions are fundamentally structured by "taste" for certain profiles, and the classification of possible partners leads individuals to contact users similar to themselves (Schmitz, 2016). Both in online environments and in interactions face to face, people engage in a mutual "spontaneous decoding," "which orient[s] social encounters, discouraging socially discordant relationships, encouraging well-matched relationships, without these operations ever having to be formulated other than in the social innocent language of likes and dislikes" (Bourdieu, 1984, p. 243).

This chapter looks into how this social selection plays out in practice. It challenges the utopian image of the internet as a space freed from social and geographical boundaries, but also the impression that a hyperselectivity based on algorithms and sorting of profiles is dominant in online interactions. More than anything, online dating brings the cultural dimensions of class distinction to the fore.

Online homogamy

An important body of academic literature has been written on *homogamy* in online dating. Homogamy is the propensity to form a couple with someone similar to oneself. The question is whether dating platforms encourage or diminish diversity. Surveys from different countries show fairly consistent results on this topic and reveal that tendencies differ depending on the type of characteristics we look at.

Age homogamy is shown to be stronger among couples that meet through a dating platform than among partners who meet in physical settings. This is the case in the United

Class at First Sight 101

States (Thomas, 2020), in Switzerland (for sites but not for apps; see Potârcă 2020), and in France, where the age gap between partners who know each other from a dating site is 1.9 years, by comparison to the 2.3 years average (Bergström, 2018). Racial homogamy has received attention primarily in the United States, where studies tend to focus on differences between physical encounters and digital encounters as a whole (rather than dating platforms specifically). It turns out that, in the United States, couples that start online are more often interracial than couples that start by meeting in person (Potârcă, 2017; Thomas, 2020). In a country where racial segregation is extremely salient, digital platforms create more diversity than the physical world. In Europe measures are different, and so are the results. In terms of migratory background, no difference is found between online and other couples, either in France or in Switzerland: partners who meet through online dating are just as likely as others to have one partner born in a foreign country (Bergström, 2019; Potârcă, 2020).

When it comes to social homogamy, sociologist Reuben J. Thomas found that there was no "difference between online and offline-formed couples in their closeness on the educational scale," although relationships that stem from online dating have a higher probability of consisting of one partner with a college degree and another without (Thomas, 2020, p. 1275). A similar result was found in Switzerland, where couples who met through a dating app were more likely to consist of one partner with tertiary education and another with non-tertiary education. But no such difference in educational homogamy was found between partners who met in person and partners who met through a dating site (Potârcă, 2020). In France, social differences are marginal. Whether you look at homogamy in education, in occupations, or in parental occupations, there is no difference between dating sites and other settings, except for people who meet in the workplace or at school and who, for obvious reasons, are more likely than others to find partners with similar jobs or credentials (Bergström, 2016a). So, apart from these work- and school-related encounters, online dating is not, in terms of social homogamy, significantly different from dating in other venues (see also Potârcă, 2017).

102   The New Laws of Love

Whether stronger or weaker than homogamy among couples whose members first met in person, the predilection for similar partners is palpable online. This is clear when we turn from surveys to big data from dating platforms. Studies on user behavior show that people interact primarily with individuals who resemble them. For instance, similarity in educational attainment significantly increases the probability to contact or respond to another user (Skopek et al., 2011), and this is particularly true of people at the extreme ends, that is, with either low or high degrees (Bergström, 2016a). A similar pattern is found for race. In *The Dating Divide*, three American sociologists present a fine-grained analysis of racial contact patterns on a major US platform, showing that homophily is strong. Users tend to engage in in-group inter-actions and "among all the racial preferences [they] find in online dating, none is stronger than Whites' preferences for Whites" (Vaughan Curington et al., 2021, p. 101; see also Lin and Lundquist, 2013). The authors also find that black women are particularly disadvantaged in online dating, whereas white men are in the most favorable position, even more so than white women (Vaughan Curington et al., 2021).

These studies point to the selective nature of the digital choice of partners. Far from pairing users at random, online dating is characterized by assortative matching. How does this process work in a setting that is so different from ordinary meeting venues? A first clue lies in the segmentation of dating platforms.

Segregation and algorithms

Segregation is not restricted to the physical world but applies to digital networks as well. This is true of racial segregation, which has characterized online dating from the outset, as platforms target different ethnic groups (see chapter 2). Sites and apps are also subject to social segregation. Several niche platforms offer their services to "high-quality singles [...] who are ambitious, driven, successful, attractive" (Luxy)[1] and who would "like to meet someone smart enough to know how to look good in a black and white photo, thoughtful enough to use proper punctuation, and understanding of your way-too-restrictive work schedule" (The League).[2] The audience targeted by these euphemisms is evident from questions about jobs and education as well as from membership charges, which are higher than on mainstream platforms. Some of these platforms operate as private communities where "prospective members may download the app and submit an application" (Raya).[3] Just as in the physical world, social boundaries are drawn by the upper classes as they establish socially distinctive spaces or even gated communities online.

Social segregation is also fueled by a "class flight" whereby the middle and upper classes abandon platforms that have become socially diverse. Interviews reveal that, whenever an app or site becomes popular, privileged users tend to migrate to newer, more selective platforms:

INTERVIEWER: What apps are you currently using?
ALIX: Right now I like happn, and Bumble is also good. It's kind of a matter of trends. What I do is I change whenever a trend stops being new. Because the longer you wait, the longer an app has been around, the more fake profiles and creeps you'll find on it; that's my impression. The quality deteriorates every time. So as soon as there's something better I switch. The first one I tried was Tinder because I thought it was good, but it turned out to be trash, really.
INTERVIEWER: What do you mean by that?
ALIX: It was a popular thing, and with popular things you get fake profiles, weird people. It's less selective actually. (Alix, 21, student; mother: housewife; father: lawyer)

When Tinder was introduced in 2012, smartphone use was still marked by a digital divide. In France, 62% of individuals with a university degree had used mobile internet in 2012, by comparison with only 17% of those with no more than primary education (Gombault, 2013). An American survey phrased its question differently, but the results are strikingly similar: 61% of the American adults with a college degree owned a smartphone in 2012, versus 21% of those with no high school diploma (Pew Research Center, 2012). The democratization of smartphones led to more specialized dating apps, which target young executives and upper-class

104 The New Laws of Love

kids. While Tinder keeps things simple and displays all its users with just a photo, other applications add job and school information (Bumble), ask questions about education and leisure, and promise "quality over quantity"[4] (Once). Certain users abandoned old platforms for new ones. As early adopters of new technologies, the upper classes are always one step ahead, ready to jettison whatever instruments are taken up by the masses and replace them with newer ones. As danah boyd established, the same phenomenon has been witnessed in social media, from MySpace to Facebook and Instagram: all were embraced by the upper classes to begin with, then lost much of their social appeal when they started to attract a wider audience (boyd, 2008, 2011). The internet has not abolished borders or frontiers; it has invented digital ones of its own.

Algorithms are another type of device that operates segregation within platforms. Far from discovering other users by chance, searchers are presented with profiles in an order of priorities. For instance, many platforms primarily display users of a similar age, who live in the same geographic area, and who are currently online. It is often claimed that this preselection of prospective partners is discriminative and responsible for much of the racial and social selection in digital dating. My research leads me to a more nuanced conclusion. I carried out an analysis of a rating system present on several Meetic Group platforms that works much like the one on dating apps such as Tinder. Users are presented, in linear succession, with profiles that they can either select or reject by pushing on a "yes" button (symbolized by a heart) or a "no" button (symbolized by a cross).

It turns out that the algorithms are in fact less selective than the users. Whereas the platforms present men with women both taller and shorter than them, male users predominantly select shorter women; and the opposite trend characterizes female behavior. People also tend to select partners with a similar education more often than the programmed algorithm does; and users who describe themselves as "European" are significantly less likely to signal interest in a person who describes her- or himself as "African," for instance. I also find that users are much more selective about age than the algorithm is: male users tend to select younger women, and female users older men, more often than if they had simply followed the platform's proposals.[5] In other words, traditional sorting criteria – which produce racial and social homogamy, or couples in which men are taller and older than their partners – are strong on dating platforms, but this is not due to algorithms as much as to users' personal choices and decisions. Research on other platforms, like Facebook and music streaming services, shows similar results, indicating that individual choice rather than algorithmic framing is the main explanatory factor in what people do online (Bakshy et al., 2015; Beuscart et al., 2019).

The rest of this chapter will focus on class dynamics in online dating. It traces the entire process of digital dating, which breaks down into three distinct phases: evaluation of user profiles; written communication; and the physical meeting. Each of these stages is characterized by specific, socially differentiated selection mechanisms, which put an end to some contacts and take others to the next level.

Distinctive profiles: photos and wordplay

To present oneself in a positive light, with just enough spice to arouse interest and intrigue but without boasting or going overboard – this is the uncomfortable challenge facing anyone who wants to create an online dating profile. Two fears must be confronted: the fear of coming across as trite or vain, and the fear of being ridiculous. Needless to say, the outcome is fairly conventional: there are codes and ways of going about things, and profiles tend to look pretty much alike. This was already the case with personal ads, as sociologist François de Singly observed in the 1980s. To those who waxed ironical about the sheer conventionality of ads, Singly explained that the task in hand "differs from a literary competition; it may not be in the advertiser's interest to seek originality at all costs," but rather to convey "impressions of normality" (Singly, 1984, p. 525). Given that in a classified ad every word counts (and costs), and given the taboo that surrounds this form of courtship, advertisers had to reassure prospective spouses that they were "just ordinary people," sound of body and mind. Online dating is more common and

106 The New Laws of Love

less suspect than matrimonial ads, but users must still prove that they are normal and likable, not too desperate, not too uptight, and especially not "crazy." Even today, conventionality is the price to pay for an "impression of normality."

This suggests a code of conduct governing self-presentation online; but, rather than a single code, there are several that coexist. Female and male profiles are not gauged the same way, and therefore women and men present themselves differently. But the codes are also socially marked. How users create their profiles, the information they provide, and the qualities they seek to highlight will vary depending on their economic and cultural capital. The interview excerpted here, with a male student, sheds light on the social judgments at work in appraising and decoding online profiles.

> COLIN: I "like" girls who are attractive, or with a funny description...
> INTERVIEWER: What do you mean by a funny description?
> COLIN: I like good cultural references. References to films can be funny. I like bad puns; I think: she's got a sense of humor, so that's good, it'll be fun. I also look at the content of the pictures, not just the person, to see how the picture was taken.
> INTERVIEWER: Have you noticed some things you like more than others?
> COLIN: There's one thing I don't like, for instance, it's like ten selfies in a row, you know, with a duck face like that [he mimics a pout and laughs]. It's horrible to mock them, but it's like, "well, you're so in love with yourself, but..." So ... I'm not going to "like" a girl, even if she's very attractive; it's simply that I find it ridiculous. [...] Some things I like... I like beautiful photos actually, photographs that were taken properly, not overfiltered from Instagram but just a pretty photo. There was one that really stood out for me, with lots of things I liked. It was a woman who was sitting by her piano, it was a black and white photo, not a photo that had been edited, it was a camera that took black and white pictures. Very attractive. She had her back to the camera. I think there was a cat on the piano, and she had a super attractive tattoo, everything was perfectly symmetrical. And the photo reached out to me, and I "liked" her. (Colin, 22, student; parents: salespeople)

As a student at a music conservatoire and hence in a situation of ascending social mobility vis-à-vis his parents (on whose low cultural capital he commented during the interview), Colin pays close attention to photographs, which he judges not only as the portrait of a person but also for their intrinsic artistry, which is revealed in composition, exposure, and the type of camera used. In comparing two types of pictures, he contrasts the sophistication of one photo to the vulgarity of selfies and mimicking "duck faces." His narrative reflects the multiple judgments of taste that come into play when we look at a photo. Far from presenting only the physical aspect of the person, which is already eminently social, the picture tells a great deal about that person's social position and lifestyle (Ward, 2017).

This is clear from a systematic analysis I carried out on photos posted on a popular dating app. Snapshots bear witness to divergent aesthetic standards and, whether intentionally or unconsciously, the subjects reveal considerable information about their social status and living conditions. Many profile photos posted by users with little economic and cultural capital were selfies taken with a smartphone at home that showed the subject smiling into the camera lens, with the domestic environment – bedroom, kitchen or bathroom – in the background. Unlike these images, which seem to have been taken on the fly, the portraits of users from privileged classes are more sophisticated – for example they appear to have been taken with a real camera, or posted in black and white – and have a more deliberate composition. Assuming a serious pose and looking away from the lens, users present themselves in settings that signal their leisure and social activities: at a café, on holiday, or playing a musical instrument. On careful examination, the photographs show the work that went into making them look spontaneous. Going beyond what Pierre Bourdieu called the "'functional' aesthetic" characteristic of the working classes (Bourdieu, 1990, p. 86), whose snapshots have the sole purpose of self-presentation, these photographs depict users in natural or nonchalant poses and at the same time provide an additional message about their tastes, their pastimes, and their territories.

Class distinctions come into play in the written part of the profile as well. In the same interview Colin stressed the

108 The New Laws of Love

importance of the "description," something the upper classes are particularly attentive to. Even a concise bio can be rich in cultural references and exhibit puns or other wordplay that individuals put in to distinguish themselves from the mass of registered users. Confident in their writing skills, the upper classes play out and enjoy displaying their cultural capital by crafting descriptions that, in many cases, simply cannot be decoded without the requisite cultural keys. Users from less privileged backgrounds, on the other hand, often post far more modest bios – or none at all. To make a written self-presentation is considered not only difficult but also pretentious.

> I left it blank. Some people write a presentation, but like two pages! [...] I gave it some thought, but it was hard, and I asked myself how I was going to post something in there. I just couldn't! [...] So I thought: no, it would only make me look foolish. (Fatima, 34, social worker)

These differing attitudes toward the written self-presentation reflect contrasting social attitudes vis-à-vis the act of writing, but also vis-à-vis the self-exposure that writing involves. This is not only about linguistic proficiency, but also about the degree to which people are prepared to put themselves on display. What does this mean for users? Because of the distinct social codes governing self-presentation, users will ignore profiles that are radically different from their own or dismiss them as incomplete, unappealing, bizarre, ridiculous, boastful, or vulgar – and they will focus instead on people who present themselves "well" according to their own standards.

Cultural prerequisites

A user from a different social class is not necessarily "swiped left," that is, rejected. Many interviewees stress that they interact with "all types, from every social and cultural background" (Virginie, 29, social worker) and that online dating makes you "talk to people you might not naturally speak with" (Audrey, 22, student; parents: bank executives).

Crucially, while users may *begin* conversations with people from different social backgrounds, they *stay in contact* mainly with those who resemble them. This trend was found in Andreas Schmitz's study of a German dating site (Schmitz, 2012), as well as in contact behavior displayed on Meetic in France (Bergström, 2016a). It means that online homogamy is not due to mere profile preselection; it develops through interaction as well.

Courtship in online dating is to some extent specific to this context. Contrary to ordinary dating, which often involves other activities such as dining, drinking, dancing, and so on, online interactions are initially strictly limited to a verbal exchange, and even that is without face-to-face communication or body language. This can make courtship more of an "intellectual, not sensory" experience, as one user readily described his initial meeting with his future spouse:

> In just a few minutes we were having a real conversation! We were immediately on another planet, equal to equal, as I said earlier. [...] You asked me earlier what kind of things Agnes and I talked about. I don't know... we talked about everything! But every topic was something that we wanted to talk about together. (Claude, 57, senior civil servant)

The affinity people feel on dating platforms reflects a verbally constructed understanding. For two users to continue their conversation beyond the initial contact, they must, as Claude points out, have "things to say to each other." What begins as a simple question-and-answer ritual can continue only if the interlocutors find a subject they are both familiar with and willing to discuss. At this stage, questions often involve what the other person does (study or work) and what the other person likes (hobbies, pastimes and passions, or tastes in music, films, or literature). The communication is facilitated if both share the same interests and, more broadly, the same referential universe. This explains why the kind of homogamy observed in online dating often accompanies cultural affinities. This is not limited to the upper classes, whose conspicuous cultural consumption sets the standard by which they judge one another, but extends to people from less privileged backgrounds, whose tastes are different but

110   The New Laws of Love

who are just as likely to talk about things they like. Brigitte's narrative shows how affinities can emerge when one person's tastes find a sympathetic response:

> He's passionate about [rockstar] Johnny Hallyday. [laughs] And as I like Johnny too... He may not be my favorite idol, but I do like him. And because he absolutely loves Johnny, he was happy to meet someone who thinks the same way, because not everyone appreciates Johnny [...] We were like on the same wavelength. (Brigitte, 50, registered nurse)

Affinity often arises from a free-flowing, reciprocating exchange where the topics of conversation come naturally. As Cécila says, "it's when you're talking with someone and there are no awkward pauses, and you know what to say; you're pretty much speaking the same language" (39, secretary). In a setting where it's not possible to share an activity, a glance, or a gesture of physical intimacy, affinity arises primarily from sharing a common universe. Humor plays a central role in developing this sense of complicity. Many users insist on the importance of irony, jokes, and puns. Shared laughter creates empathy, while a joke that falls flat is often met with awkward silence. Humor is eminently social, being based on a system of references that must be shared if the meaning is to be grasped. As such, it also contributes to social homogamy.

Cultural affinity, as we have seen, is closely tied to social self-selection; but this is only one side of the process. Rejection – the elimination of unsuitable partners – is another element of online exchange. While members of all social groups – executives and manual workers alike – show an inclination for partners who resemble them, the practices of disqualifying another are much more one-sided, and they are directed at people in a lower position in the social hierarchy. This social rejection is plainly visible in the vehement dislike of poor spelling.

The diffusion of mobile apps has by no means diminished the key role played by the written word in online dating. Profiles are now more visual and less verbal, but communication is still based on text: people don't speak online; they write. This was obviously the case in the early days, when the internet was a text-based virtual world, and it remains

Class at First Sight 111

unchanged today, on multimedia platforms. Mobile phones are now used less for calling and more for texting. While most people in the western world can read and write, their language and writing skills vary considerably. This is particularly the case with speakers of languages like French, where spelling follows complicated rules of grammar and is rarely phonetic (Bernstein, 1975; Lahire, 2008).

The implication is simple but crucial: online dating is built upon a highly discriminatory mode of communication, in which writing is much more than just a medium. Spelling turns out to be a criterion of selection for users with a higher education, regardless of their degree, level, or academic discipline. It is also the only social criterion that is bluntly admitted as such. These two interviewees make it clear: "if someone can't spell, there's no chance!" (Yannick, 31, secondary school teacher). "If I see spelling mistakes, I'll move on directly" (Élodie, 20, student; mother: secondary school teacher; father: engineering manager). Because writing is intimately but only implicitly linked to social class, users have no problem with expressing their dislike, or even their contempt.

PATRICK: If someone's not good at spelling and grammar, that's a nonstarter. A total nonstarter. [...].
INTERVIEWER: You wouldn't meet up with her?
PATRICK: I wouldn't meet up with her. Wrongly maybe, but for me spelling is clearly linked to two things that are interconnected. And that's one's upbringing, and one's level – not necessarily intellectual level, because that's something else. Poor spelling isn't a matter of intellectual level but of upbringing. And that doesn't correspond to my values either. Even if I'm French, I make the effort at school to learn spelling, and how to speak correctly. I hope I speak correctly. So, for people who haven't made that effort, well that's that. (Patrick, 32, consultant)

DELPHINE: I've had conversations with people who were very different. A firefighter, who seemed very young but was actually about my own age. One who was in IT, I think. And then there was one who was in aeronautics and one who was in catering, an oenologist or something like that. So, between the fireman who was adorable but couldn't spell, who spoke like a really young person, I

112 The New Laws of Love

> just gave up [...] We wrote quite a lot of emails to each other. The reason I finally gave up on him, I admit, was his language... he really wrote like someone in the first grade! [laughter]. (Delphine, 32, social worker)

Condescending attitudes toward culturally underprivileged users are common. Judgments related to writing encompass the entire social hierarchy in values expressed by opposites: mature–immature, well educated–crude, serious–lazy, intelligent–stupid, refined–vulgar, and so on. Social distance takes the form of moral distance: the behaviors of the working classes, and especially their language, are considered to be lacking in "value" (Le Wita, 1988). Spelling – as a distinctive practice – reveals a certain "linguistic insecurity" (Bretegnier and Ledegen, 2002), especially that of the French middle classes, whose members seek to establish their social status through command of the French language. But the importance of good spelling has also been observed in other countries, for instance in the Netherlands (Ward, 2017).

These social judgments do not apply only to serious or romantic relationships. Poor spelling may totally rule out even a casual fling, as this respondent points out: "If I see she can't spell, or basically that she doesn't know how to write, it's not possible. Even if it's just for sex [...] I couldn't do it" (Paul, 26, web marketing manager). A common assumption (even among sociologists) is that the social characteristics valued in a life partner differ radically from expectations from a casual partner, because couple formation has far more important consequences than casual sex. But this assumption overlooks the fact that all forms of dating call upon judgments of taste (likes and dislikes) about what is beautiful, ugly, refined, ridiculous, or vulgar, that is, they call upon socially constructed perceptions. This explains why hookups, and even escorting, are subject to assortative logics, both online and not (Laumann et al., 1994; Rubio, 2013; Nasser, 2020).

Codes of conduct

Courtship is usually approached through the prism of gender, but it is also a social practice and, as such, a means of social

Class at First Sight   *113*

differentiation and distinction. The dating game is played differently according to social class, since the rules are not the same. This is clear from the messages that users send each other and from their topics of conversation. Although getting to know each other better is the general aim of online inter-action, there are different opinions about what information ought to be shared in a dating context. Interviews show a particularly sharp contrast in attitudes toward discussing matters of intimacy in the earlier phases of interaction. While previous experiences and immediate expectations are major topics of conversation for users from lower middle-class and working-class backgrounds, such topics seem totally incon-gruous to socially privileged users.

> So, you ask about being single or not, and people go like "how long have you been single? I've been single for so and so, and you?" And yeah, you also talk about why things didn't work out with your ex. I think people ask this question in order to see if the other person has a problem. (Jennifer, 23, student; mother: cleaner; father: foreman)

> Hold on: I remember a guy asking something like: How many guys have you been with? Something along those lines. Right away, in the first message! That's kind of...! Hold on, take your time, ask me what I do in life and things like that. Yes, often it's something along those lines, about past relationships or things like that [...] [It's weird] that a guy who's interested in me says: "Yeah, how many relationships did you have?"... You see what I mean! (Sarah, 23, student; mother: translator; father: graphic designer)

Even on a platform explicitly devoted to dating, topics involving partner preference and relationship experiences are considered off limits by socially privileged users. While dating involves showing interest in the other person, asking about sex and love is not deemed appropriate at an early stage.

Dating codes also differ in how people show their appre-ciation. Users from working-class backgrounds say that compliments are central to courtship. For one respondent, complimenting is central to the dating game as it "makes things move forward, like: 'I really like you,' 'you're charming,' 'you're beautiful,' and things like that" (Karim, 24,

114 The New Laws of Love

student; mother: unemployed caregiver; father: unknown).
For another, it's quite the opposite: a man "who's in a hurry
to convey that he likes you" is "vulgar" and "lacking in tact"
(Audrey, 22, student; parents: bank executives). Whereas in
the working classes courtship protocol demands that interest
in the other person be articulated explicitly, the middle
and upper classes prize the ambiguity of intentions, using
unspoken hints and cues that require reading between the
lines.

These contrasts in styles of courtship are directly linked
to different social environments. The dating geography in
physical space is socially segregated: people from the upper
classes more often get to know their partners in closed or
private environments (such as parties, work, or school) while
people from the lower classes often meet their partners in a
public place (in the street, at a bar, in the mall, etc.) (Bozon
and Rault, 2012; Lampard, 2007). With these different
contexts come different forms of courtship. The dating game
of the socially privileged, which is characterized by ambiguity
and things left unspoken, is played out in environments
where the protagonists are bound to meet again and where
a curious audience, in the form of mutual acquaintances and
friends, may be attending the scene. This largely explains the
cautious nature of flirting in these social groups.

The tentative approach characteristic of the privileged
classes is much less suited to a public space – which is where
people from the working classes more often meet. In a public
place, the challenge is not only to attract the other person's
attention, but also to make sure that there will be a second
meeting, one that otherwise may not take place. The scene of
interaction then forces the actors, especially the men, who are
expected to take the initiative, to "show their cards." In other
words, there is little room for subtlety in settings like the
street, or public transport, for example – where it is necessary
to signal one's interest. These dating codes, produced by
different experiences of meeting venues, are imported online,
where they lead users to interact in very different ways.

INTERVIEWER: What do they say?
VANESSA: "Hey beautiful, how are you? You've got a lovely
smile, you've got a nice profile, what do you do for a

Class at First Sight

living, where do you live?" Well, something like that. (Vanessa, 31, waitress)

SARAH: They say you've got a beautiful name, but they're not interested in what you do. You say to yourself it's totally absurd, you know. It's something like, you're smiling in the picture, so they'll say "You've got a lovely smile." Okay, it's nice of them, but there's nothing special about it, you know. (Sarah, 23, student; mother: translator; father: graphic designer)

Currently pursuing degrees in philosophy and the history of science, Sarah was brought up in a family with a high degree of cultural capital and wants to be valued for her intellect rather than for her smile or her first name. Unlike Vanessa in the previous quotation, she dismisses such compliments as trite and out of place. She is thoroughly invested in her studies and would prefer that boys be interested in what she does. Her comments show how important it is for her potential partner to recognize the qualities that she values in herself. Romantic and sexual preferences are relational in nature, in that they concern not only the characteristics of the partner (what we value in him or her) but also the way in which the partner reflects who we are, through his or her appreciation and person (what he or she says about us). On the internet, Sarah rejects men who fail to recognize the qualities that she considers essential to who she is, which leads her to favor men who are socially similar to her.

Dating is often described as a "game," because of its conventions and highly ritualized nature. Being able to play this game together, by the same rules, is crucial in the decision to take things to the next level: the face-to-face encounter.

Social bodies

In his study of couple formation, Michel Bozon underscored the central role of physical appearance in romantic and sexual encounters. Considered as an "overall sign" capable of revealing a person's psychological, intellectual, and social qualities, the body is the focus of judgments on potential partners and plays a crucial role in assortative matching

116   The New Laws of Love

(Bozon, 1991a). What is specific to online dating is that it postpones in-person, face-to-face interaction, moving it to a subsequent stage. This reversal of sequencing does not make the physical body less important. People anticipate, or know by experience, that the person they meet in real life may not look like the profile online, and this prompts many to speed up the first in-person meeting in order to confirm or invalidate the first impressions formed online. Co-presence is considered the only way of truly knowing whom you are dealing with.

The weight placed on meeting the other one in person is not only about looks. To reduce the body to mere aesthetics would be to overlook physical appearance as a source of judgments about the *person*. What is crucial, as one female user explained, is "everything you don't get on the internet, their body language, their reactions, and so on, which tell a lot about people" (Anna, 23, student; mother: head bookkeeper; father: HR manager). The attraction (or lack of it) goes far beyond physical appearance or sex appeal.

> INTERVIEWER: You said it takes five minutes to tell?
> SYLVIE: I would say even after a minute or two. You know, it's alchemy. You know right away whether or not you're going to like the person.
> INTERVEIWER: Because of conversation?
> SYLVIE: No, I think it's physical. It's something that either connects or it doesn't. But it has nothing to do with whether he's good-looking or not, because I've had some pretty ugly ones. It's more a kind of alchemy, something that just happens. (Sylvie, 57, economically inactive)

The physical body is the basis for multiple judgments that will determine whether or not the relationship can become intimate. Users resort to vague terms to describe what is often an immediate impression, especially when it is negative: "It's hard to describe or to know exactly what it is. But it's easy to know when it's not there" (Sandra, 24, student; parents: laboratory employees). Users describe an overall impression in which multiple factors – social, psychological, intellectual, and physical – come into play that they find hard to separate. The term "alchemy" evokes this sense of instant affinity, which has nothing biological about it but rather involves a

Class at First Sight 117

blend of different intuitive judgments. This physical accord is just as vital in online dating as in other contexts, but the body plays a slightly different role.

Even if they spend little time interacting online before meeting in person, individuals go to the first date with information about each other's characteristics; this information comes either from the profile or from written conversations. The first physical encounter is an occasion on which each person can see how the other *embodies* his or her social identity. Rather than being a basis for first impressions, the physical appearance serves here to confirm or reject earlier appreciations.

> I had met another one, but then it didn't go well because, first of all, he didn't look anything like the guy in the photos. I mean, it was him, but it didn't really match. The way he spoke to me, his attitude... It forms a whole, and there was something wrong. He came across as a little bit macho, whereas in the photos he didn't look macho at all. He was the kind of guy who thinks he's cool but isn't [she scowls]. I don't know how to explain it, but the way he sits down, he doesn't look you in the eye; there were lots of things that made me think he just wouldn't do. Also, his voice. But lots of things, there were really lots of things. His voice was a little weird [laughs]. (Carla, 22, student; parents: private sector managers)

The first in-person encounter makes users measure the distance between their mental image and the actual appearance of the other person. They also learn about his or her lifestyle, as they can size up that person not only visually but also in context. Users' narratives stress the importance of what the first date – where the two went and what they did – tells about the other person and any future relationship. This first date is often arranged in easy-to-access places such as cafés or bars, where beverages can be consumed quickly, which require little commitment in time, money, or symbolic value, and where the date can easily be terminated if need be. Subsequent dates, however, are more socially discriminating. In the upper classes, they are often organized around "legitimate" cultural practices (art exhibitions, concerts, the theater), while the middle and lower classes more often favor walks, trips to the cinema, and dinners at home. These

The New Laws of Love

settings are critical for how the other person will be judged: a good date is one that leaves a good impression of the individual, but also of the time that was spent together. By the same token, a setting that fails to meet expectations can cast an altogether negative light.

> To tell the truth, there was something... I would say "cramped." That was just my impression; it had nothing to do with him. But when he invited me to meet up at his place, I saw his apartment. Then we went to the restaurant he chose, and it was a bit stuffy and moldy. I just thought: "No, that isn't my world anymore." I just couldn't live that way. (Véronique, 68, retired head of advertising agency)

Véronique comes from a working-class family and has worked her way up the social ladder. Here she recounts her meeting with a musician she very much appreciated as a person. The relationship did not, however, outlast the first encounter, largely because of the setting. Véronique had associated the musician, a man of culture, with a certain lifestyle but he failed to meet her expectations; his world appeared "cramped" by comparison to what she expected. When two individuals meet in person for the first time, class becomes visible not only in the other person's physical body, voice, and gestures, but also in his or her social environment and practices. Here again, social affinities matter.

* * *

Online dating makes it clear that, even in a mass market, not all products are consumed in a uniform manner. Although today we buy the same goods, share musical references, and have the same digital practices, this "massification" of culture has not eliminated social differences or distinctive practices. We are seeing instead a shift in social boundaries, which now reside – more subtlety but no less effectively – in the *modes of appropriation* rather than in the *nature* of the goods and services consumed (Coulangeon, 2011).

Dating sites and apps bear witness to this in a singular way. Many of the big mainstream platforms, such as Match or Tinder, host a socially diverse population and invite users to present themselves in highly standardized profiles. Despite this apparently uniform universe, usage is socially diverse. Styles of photography, ways of writing, topics of conversation, and courtship codes are all areas where expectations and practices differ across social groups. Shared references and lifestyle activities facilitate emotional affinities, whereas differences in attitudes and behaviors produce surprises at best, and contempt at worst. It's precisely because online dating platforms are available to a vast audience, and because they present everyone as a potential partner, that they make it so clear – first and foremost to the users themselves – that not everyone makes for a "match." There are boundaries – cultural, material, and symbolic – that divide people into different classes. Far from eliminating these frontiers, online dating reveals the force and the modus operandi of assortative selection in partner choice.

In doing so, it shows that privatization does not mean deregulation. We conform to social norms and roles not because of peer pressure and external control, but primarily because of interiorized dispositions. Online dating puts the finger on what we mean by "social structures" (Schmitz, 2016). In economics writings, this term usually refers to elements external to the individual that frame and constrain his or her action. In a pioneer study of online dating, Hitsch and colleagues (2010) described structural factors in partner matching as "search frictions" that limit personal preferences and choice. Interestingly, a similar reading can be found at the opposite side of the academic spectrum, among critical theorists. According to Eva Illouz, modern society is characterized by an abundance of partner choice that results from the "collapse of religious, ethnic, racial, and class rules of endogamy" (Illouz, 2012, p. 91). Here too, structures are associated with constraint, and deregulation with choice. However, as we have seen in this chapter, even when the formal obstacles to social mixing are relaxed, homogamy tends to persist through individual action. This is because social structures do not constrain us but constitute us; they not only create obstacles but also shape our will. We are social creatures – and we continue to be so when we go online.

This is not to say that the process of partner choice is the same today as it was some fifty years ago. Broad

120 The New Laws of Love

transformations like secularization, deindustrialization, longer school enrolment, new sexual norms, and loosening family control have created new social structures and thereby changed the logic of assortative matching. Online dating is revealing of these changes; it shows the centrality of *cultural affinities* in contemporary relationships. Individuals do not necessarily seek a partner with the same credentials, or with a similar type of job; on the contrary, they may like the idea of meeting someone different from themselves. However, mutual understanding, shared values, beliefs, and interests, as well as the possibility of sharing a good laugh, are central to our modern conception of intimacy and love. These features are class-dependent: our upbringing and our background shape our way of thinking and living, which we seek to share with our partners. When we do, we feel supported, understood, and loved. Social homogamy is then reproduced, but in cultural terms more than in educational and occupational ones. Cultural affinities are the social glue of contemporary love.

6

The Age of Singles

The past five decades have seen a continuous increase in the number of singles all over Europe and North America. I use the term "single" in a broad sense, to cover all those who are not in a couple. This includes the unmarried, the divorced, and the widowed, as well as people who have never been married. The singles are numerous. In the United States, for example, the proportion of unpartnered individuals has increased over time; in 2017 it represented roughly two fifth of all adults (Fry, 2017). Two factors can explain this rise. On the one hand, the delay in the age at which young people form their first relationship extends the period of singlehood during youth. On the other hand, the increase in the rate of separations and divorce means that many women and men revert to singlehood at some stage in their lives.

Today many of these singles resort to online dating when they want to flirt, date, have casual sex, or look for a spouse. But, albeit specifically conceived of to serve the purpose of meeting partners, these platforms do not place all newcomers on an equal footing; online dating has its winners and losers. Given that sex and love are valuable goods, these differences can be read in terms of inequality, as access to these resources is not equally distributed among the population. The absence of contacts and the lack of partners is correlated

122   The New Laws of Love

with social and demographic characteristics more than just with individual difficulties.

While previous chapters have looked at different ways of entering online dating and using these platforms, this chapter turns to the question of outcomes. Who are those who take their chance on the internet, and what are the odds of their being successful? Answers to these questions can be found in big data extracted from dating platforms and in scientific surveys. Both sources point to three salient factors: age, sex, and social class. I will put particular focus on the idea of *gendered ages*: women and men of the same age are not judged in the same way and do not have the same opportunities to meet partners. These gender inequalities in ageing are nowhere more evident than in online dating.

Sex ratios and little white lies about age

Before turning to the issue of unequal probabilities of getting a date or finding a spouse, let us stop to consider the question of the unequal probabilities of being single and resorting to dating platforms. In a heterosexual setting, the chances of meeting a partner depend on the relative number of available individuals of the opposite sex. "Man drought" or "marriage squeeze" can make it difficult to get a match. What is the situation on mainstream platforms?

It is often claimed that males outnumber females on apps and sites because women are less interested in online dating than men. This opinion is widespread among males, including among the CEOs of dating companies, who see women as a "challenging" customer base insofar as they must be persuaded to join. Male users tend to agree, as some bitterly complain about "ten guys for every girl." The sex ratio of users – that is, the number of female users compared to that of male users – is actually far less unbalanced than the conventional (male) wisdom would suggest.

A greater percentage of men say they have used online dating. In the United States, the 2019 survey from the Pew Research Center found that, among American adults, 32% of men and 28% of women reported having already used a dating site or app (Pew Research Center, 2020c). This slight gender imbalance is mainly due to the over-representation of younger men, as most users of dating platforms are under 35 (see Figure 6.1). This is an age at which men are more likely than women to be single, as they typically settle down later in life. Consequently, if men outnumber women on dating platforms, the main reason is that there are more single males than single females in the age groups from which platforms primarily recruit their users. To phrase it differently, if young women use these platforms slightly less than men, it's not because they are less interested in online dating but because they are more often already in a relationship.

The situation changes as people advance in age. After 40 or 50 (depending on countries), women are more likely to be single than men and are just as likely as men – if not even more than them – to have used dating platforms (see Figure 6.1). On several Meetic Group platforms as well on other sites, as age goes up, females gradually outnumber male users. This means that the sex ratio of users follows to a degree the sex ratio of singles in the general population. Online dating is affected by the same demographic trends as society as a whole. Far from constituting a "parallel marriage market" – a term used in the past to describe personal ads and matrimonial agencies – for individuals "excluded from

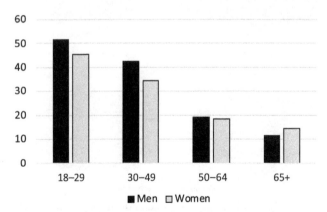

Figure 6.1. Percentage, by age group, of the women and men in the United States who have used a dating site or app at least once (%)

Scope: American adults aged 18 or more.

Source: ATP survey, wave 56 (US, 2019, Pew Research Center).

the normal marriage market" (Singly, 1984, p. 252), online dating broadly reflects the general trends that affect singles in society.

The number of women and men on dating platforms is not the only topic of debate. Age is another sensitive subject. When registering with a dating site or app, age is compulsory: it validates the user's profile and access to the platform. This information can be used to construct an age pyramid for any given year and analyze the distribution of active users according to age. Figure 6.2 shows just such an age pyramid for different European platforms, which all require users to enter their birthdate. The pyramids show that people can be flexible with the truth online. This may come as no surprise, but what is interesting is that the information entered by users is adjusted less than is usually claimed. Birth dates may simply be rounded off, as users seem to prefer numbers that are multiples of five such as 1980, 1985, 1990 or 35, 40, 45.

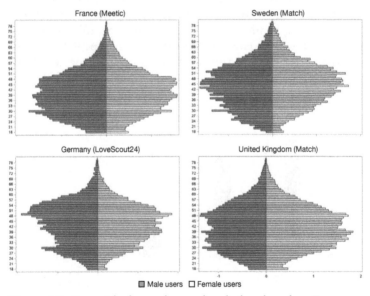

Figure 6.2. Pyramid of ages, by gender, declared on four European dating platforms (%)

Scope: Active user profiles that registered in 2019 (an "active" user is one who has sent at least one message to another user).

Source: Meetic Group Databases (Europe, 2019, Meetic Group).

The Age of Singles   125

This explains the spikes observed on either side where ages have been rounded, presumably downward. Those in their thirties seem particularly sensitive about their age, as this is where most of the rounding occurs. It is interesting to note that women do not appear to be more sensitive about their age than men are, since misstatements are recorded for both sexes.

These practices show the delicate paradox involved in "translating" one's age into a number. In in-person dating contexts, someone's chronological age is rarely known from the outset, but will be inferred from physical appearance. People who feel or look younger or more mature than the date on their passport or identity card may struggle with the idea of reducing age to the raw datum. Users of classified ads often sought to convey additional information, such as "49 but looks 40," "43, young in body and mind," and "69 but appears younger" (Fages, 1972, p. 92). This kind of embellishment is impossible on digital platforms that require a number. Users may be tempted to replace their actual age by what they consider to be their more favorable "physical" or "social" age. These stratagems show that age is more than an official figure; it is also a matter of subjective experience.

More importantly, these misrepresentations point to the central role that age plays in dating. Users change their date of birth because they anticipate the age preferences of their prospective partners. Most platforms prompt users to indicate an age range for potential partners, and this request makes some users try to satisfy the criteria they imagine other users have. These strategies were identified early on by the American researchers Nicole Ellison, Rebecca Heino, and Jennifer Gibbs, who found that people misrepresent their age in profiles primarily in order to avoid being "filtered out" by those they wish to impress. In other words, users try to game the system by tricking the filters and algorithms so as to improve their own chances. Consequently, it is not unusual for someone to reveal his or her real age as soon as contact with the prospective partner is made and conversation begins (Ellison et al., 2006).

People in a dating situation normally try to look their best in order to please the other person. In ordinary conditions, we are hardly surprised when people dress up, dye their hair,

126 The New Laws of Love

or use makeup to appear younger. On the other hand, we are often shocked when people misstate their age for the same purpose on dating platforms, as the need to use objective numerical values turns what would be mere embellishments in real life into outright lies. Several studies of the truthfulness of profiles indicate that improvements are common, but rather moderate in nature (Schmitz et al., 2011). Apart from photos, the most frequent adjustments are to age, height, and weight (Toma et al., 2008; Zillmann et al., 2011). All three of these characteristics are scale variables that change over time; variations are often not visible and adjustments may be considered unimportant. On Meetic, for instance, users are slightly taller and slimmer than the rest of the French population but the deviations from the national average are small, as both sexes are about two centimeters taller, while men and women weigh two and five kilograms less respectively (Bergström, 2018). In other words, the adjustments tend to be reasonable and the values entered online are seldom radically different from those on the weighing scale or on identity documents.

Because misrepresentations are intended to meet the preferences of others, they are more likely to occur when users feel the need to compensate for what they consider to be an imperfection. German researchers Doreen Zillman, Andreas Schmitz, and Hans-Peter Blossfeld found that having an attribute that is considered to reduce one's attractiveness (e.g. being overweight, or being short for a man) increases the likelihood of one's altering that attribute or offsetting the deficiency by enhancing other features (Zillmann et al., 2011). This means that misrepresentation is neither systematic nor done at random. In fact lies are the weapon of the weak. While users who conform to conventional standards of beauty and social status can afford to be "honest," those who recognize a flaw in themselves are more likely to embellish their self-presentation. This is another lesson from attempts to doctor profiles: not everyone is equal before the laws of love. The ability to establish contacts and meet people varies from one group to another. The most striking inequalities are those related to age, which imposes upper and lower limits; there are ages when one is too young, too old, undesirable, not yet acceptable, disqualified, or simply ignored.

Waiting young men, pickup artists, and incels

Not everyone who uses online dating sites and apps will actually find a date or a mate. This is primarily the case for young men who are largely ignored by women of the same age. By comparison with other users of dating platforms, men under the age of 25 are at a distinct disadvantage, many of them being effectively excluded from online interactions. This is evident on Meetic Group platforms, where the initial messages sent by males under 25 receive considerably less attention than the messages sent by older male users. Similarly, young men are the least likely to be directly contacted by women.[1]

Interviews also show that many young men simply stop using online dating services after failing to make any real connections. Bertrand, a 22-year-old student, discusses his inability to meet girls; and because he is also looking to meet boys, he observes that young women are far less likely to respond to his "likes" than male users of the same age.

> If it's girls, I immediately swipe right, because you can sort through the matches later, and I don't get that many. I think that all guys do that, right? With girls, I swipe right and sort later, because my chance of getting a match with a girl is fairly low. I've got a lot of friends who are struggling; there's one who must have been on Tinder for the past two years, with maybe ten matches with girls. [...] My only matches are with guys. But if I put in that I'm looking only for girls, I won't have any matches at all. (Bertrand, 22, student; mother: company owner; father: skilled worker)

Because of the low female response rate, young heterosexual men try to initiate contact with a large number of women, often indiscriminately and without spending much time selecting the profiles to contact (Tyson et al., 2016). The tactic is common and hardly successful. It is this paucity of responses that fuels the perception, strong among young men, that male users outnumber female users by ten to one, as one in ten messages receives a reply (on average). The imbalance between invitations and responses is responsible for the impression that the demographic imbalance between

128 The New Laws of Love

the sexes is even greater than it is. Nadir, like many other disappointed young men, admits that he has never met anyone in person:

> NADIR: My impression is that men outnumber women by so much on Tinder and Badoo, that women sort through them pretty fast. And because I'm not good at writing, it's not my messages that will get me noticed [...]
> INTERVIEWER: Have you ever met any in real life?
> NADIR: No, not many. Actually, no one. (Nadir, 18, high-school student;' mother: cleaner; father: unknown)

The reason why young heterosexual men have trouble attracting attention, making contacts, and meeting women in person is that female users of the same age turn to older men. This trend can be observed in all dating situations, both online and not. Early in their life, women express a clear preference for older partners, and when they form a couple the man is generally older. The age gap between spouses is a particularly strong demographic trend all around the world (Mignot, 2010; Giuliani, 2020). In France, for instance, the male spouse is on average two years older than the female spouse (Bergström, 2018).[2]

In his research on couple formation in the 1980s, Michel Bozon pointed to young women's "categorical rejection" of men of their age, who are considered to be "kids," "naïve," "too young," or "silly," in other words, too "immature in their behavior and their preoccupations" (Bozon, 1991c, p. 127). Women, when forming their first relationships, prefer more mature men, in established social positions, and with a degree of economic and residential independence. Maturity here is less a matter of chronological than of social age. Older men are considered "mature," primarily because they have the experience and stability to provide a sense of security, including emotional security (Bozon, 1991c).

Forty years after Bozon's study, the premium placed on older men seems as strong as ever. This is evident in many of the interviews with young women. Melissa, for example, discusses here her last date with a young man she met on an app whom she considers shallow and lacking in initiative and explains her preference for older men:

The Age of Singles 129

It's been some time since I met anyone new; the last one, his name was was Nicolas. He's pretty young, actually too young for me [laughs]. Because I am used to having men who were really older, more mature, who had considerable life experience, when I'm with a young guy like that, it bores me. Even conversation-wise, they don't have much to say from which I learn new things. It depends, but in any case, the last one I saw, Nicolas, I thought he was a bit hollow, two-dimensional. I was the one who was making conversation [...] I expect the guy to take charge of things, from start to finish, to behave like a real man. And that's why things are generally more awkward with guys my own age, or from 21 to 24, because they're not used to it; they have less experience. (Melissa, 21, student; mother: librarian; father: special needs educator)

This woman's expectations reveal a profound asymmetry. Melissa asks men to direct the conversation and take charge "from start to finish." She herself is still a student but her partner must have "life experience." This type of relationship scenario is far removed from the image of the modern couple as a "pure relationship [that] cannot exist without substantial elements of reciprocity" (Giddens, 1992, p. 93). The ideal relationship described by Anthony Giddens is far more symmetrical than the one captured by many young women's narratives, where the man is expected to take the lead and take care of his partner. There is something astonishing about the enduring power of this traditional vision of the couple, in which men are supposed to take the lead, protect women, and see to their needs. Women as a group have experienced significant social mobility over the past decades; in many western countries they are today more highly educated than men, participate fully in the labor market, work in skilled professions, and are increasingly gaining access to positions of authority. And yet they seem to have some reluctance about extending their hard-earned independence to the romantic sphere. When choosing a partner, many young women look less for reciprocity than for support and security, and therefore turn to older men.

This female preference for "maturity" means that young men find themselves left out and must wait until they reach

130   The New Laws of Love

an age that will make them more eligible and appealing as partners. Prospects improve with age, with more contacts, with more in-person dates, and as more men have romantic and sexual experiences. The interactional data from the Meetic Group platforms testify to the fact that the success rate of male contacts increases with age. Surveys give a very similar picture; in the United States for instance, 66% of men aged between 18 and 30 in 2019 declared that they had gone at least once on a date with a person they first met on a dating app or site, by comparison with 81% of the men aged between 30 and 64.[3] The question was phrased differently in the French EPIC survey, but points in the same direction: in 2013, 57% of the 26–30-year-old male users of online dating reported that they had had a sexual or a romantic relationship with a person known from online dating, by comparison with 77% of men in the 56–60 age group, for example.[4] For young men, dating is a waiting game.

Some young men take the female rejection badly, all the more because of the traditional gender hierarchy: there are few situations in which men feel so demeaned by women and at the same time so dependent on their will. A situation like this tends to generate frustration, and even resentment. This is clear from the "seduction community," a brotherhood that gained visibility in 2005, with the publication of Neil Strauss's (2005) book *The Game*, and that has since reached a broad audience, both in North America and in Europe. The seduction community operates both online and in physical space and relies on professional pickup artists to teach other men how to be successful with women. Research on the phenomenon predominantly insists on the ideology of male domination and female objectification that the community conveys (O'Neill, 2015; Gourarier, 2017), but some studies also emphasize the isolation and loneliness of its members (Whitley and Zhou, 2020). These two aspects are not in conflict, on the contrary. As Jitse Schuurmans and Lee F. Monaghan stressed in their study of the seduction community in California, the brotherhood "with its hyper-masculine and conservative folk beliefs was particularly seductive for sexually inexperienced and/or socially isolated young men who felt out of control, lonely, inept and adrift" (Schuurmans and Monaghan, 2015, p. 104).

The Age of Singles   *131*

There are parallels between the seduction community and the movement of a group of men known as "incels" (involuntary celibates), although the latter is characterized by a more extreme misogyny and has been linked to violent crimes against women, especially in the United States. The incels cultivate hatred of women, whom they blame for their romantic and sexual failures. These movements have been justly described as antifeminist movements. But this should not make us shy away from the fact that the misogynist outburst is a sign of the rejection and failure that some men feel when excluded from any semblance of intimacy. Far from suggesting that women are to blame (as the incels assert when urging men to reclaim their rightful access to female bodies), this acknowledgment shows that even the most reprehensible phenomena have a sociological explanation. The seduction community, and even more so the incels' movement, are rather marginal phenomena, but they shed light on the issues that face men in early adulthood. Indeed, most of the men who learn skills to attract women or spread hate against them online are young. Their resentment is age-related and does not necessarily reflect a general trend of rising "masculinism" in the general population. Nevertheless, this age-specific form of machismo reveals how unexpected – and unacceptable – it is for men to be dismissed by women in a world still defined by a strong gender hierarchy.

Waiting to get a date and longing to catch the interest of girls is a common experience for many young men. When the period is long or lasts for a lifetime, the experience is also socially situated.

The new bachelors' ball

In *The Bachelors' Ball*, Pierre Bourdieu (2008) described the transformation from rural to urban society and the men who were left behind. The protagonists in this social history are peasants who were destined to inherit as elder sons of landowning farming families, yet whose social status fell drastically at the turn of the twentieth century. Their privileged position in rural society meant that they were traditionally the first to marry, and yet a growing number of

132   The New Laws of Love

them remained single. Women left the countryside, preferring to marry men in steady employment. Urbanization, economic change, and female education had made women more mobile, and also more capable of adapting to a new, urban lifestyle. As a result, women were "reluctant to marry a peasant who offers them exactly what they want[ed] to escape from" (Bourdieu, 2008, p. 183). Out of step with the values and practices of their time, these rural men had been left behind. Nowhere is their marginalization more poignantly depicted than in the scene from a Christmas ball in the back room of a village café. At the center of the room young women from the countryside dance with young men from town, while the rural men stand together away from the bright lights, ignored and unmarriageable: "the bachelors will remain there, until midnight, hardly speaking, in the light and noise of the ball, gazing at the girls beyond their reach" (p. 83).

The village dances have disappeared and farmer numbers have dwindled. But Bourdieu's bachelors, the men who are left behind, are still with us. While it is generally rare today, for both sexes, to never experience a significant romantic relationship in the course of one's lifetime, a non-negligible proportion of men from poor and working-class backgrounds will never have this experience. In France, among men aged 40 and over, only a small minority of those in intermediate and higher professions say that they have never had a such a romantic relationship (3%), whereas the situation is more common among farmers (16%), manual workers (9%), and men in sales-related occupations (7%). Men in these categories are also more likely to have never had a cohabiting union. This is the case for 19% of farmers, 15% of manual workers, and 12% of men in sales-related occupations aged 40 or over – by comparison with only 3% of men of the same age in executive and higher professions.[5]

The same inequalities arise when comparing men's educational attainment: those with low educational qualifications are the least likely to report having experienced a significant intimate relationship, let alone cohabitation. Social inequalities reflected in couple formation are less pronounced among women, who now have a higher educational level than their male peers in many western countries (Breen et al., 2010). As the levels of education have risen across the population,

The Age of Singles   *133*

especially for women, poorly educated men with low skills are increasingly disadvantaged – both on the labor market and in the intimate sphere. This social divide in matters of love has increased over time, as Milan Bouchet-Valat demonstrates in a study of the historical links between education and singlehood in France. For men, the risk of lifelong singlehood (defined here as having never lived with someone in a couple) has become increasingly class-dependent. Among Frenchmen born in the 1920s, this risk was low and equal for all, regardless of educational level; but social contrasts have risen gradually, so that men born fifty years later, in the 1970s, who left school without a diploma or with no more than a primary school certificate were significantly less likely than the better educated ones to have lived in a cohabiting union (Bouchet-Valat, 2015).

This means that some men are totally excluded from intimate relationships, and increasingly so. Out of step with a highly educated society, a significant minority of socially disadvantaged men are devalued not only by employers but also by potential partners. This exclusion operates on dating sites too, as the EPIC survey shows: among French male users, those from executive and higher professions are almost twice as likely as workers to have experienced a romantic or a sexual relationship via a dating platform.[6] Online dating is not a magic solution for singles; many of those who are already at a disadvantage in ordinary dating often meet with disappointment on the internet as well. The same holds for women, although single women face an entirely different set of inequalities.

Gender inequalities in aging

With age, the balance between men and women shifts in terms of opportunities to meet a partner. In France, from the age of 25 to the age of 40, both sexes have roughly the same chance of a sexual or romantic experience through online dating, but after that things change. Whereas men older than 40 are more likely than younger men to meet someone online, women older than 40 are less likely than younger women, and also than men of their own age, to have a sexual

134   The New Laws of Love

or romantic experience through a dating site.[7] The explanation is to be found in the *gendering of ages*: aspirations and dating opportunities change over the course of a lifetime, but in different ways for women and men.

As women grow older, the premium they place on older men decreases significantly. After the age of 30, women treat men of their own age as valued partners rather than as outcasts. Men have moved beyond the uncertainties associated with early adulthood (e.g. studies and career instability) and no longer need to prove themselves. And women, having gained experience, have a more pragmatic attitude toward romantic relationships.

This is particularly true after a breakup. The experience of having lived in a couple, especially if there are children, changes what women expect from a partner and what future they imagine for themselves. While young women tend to have an idealistic view on couple life, older women express their expectations with realism, and sometimes with a touch of disenchantment. A case in point is Patricia, who registered on Meetic after her divorce. When asked to describe what she looks for in a future partner, she answers briefly, then dwells at length on what she wants to avoid: someone with children and an overhanging relationship from his past. After a failed marriage that left her with two dependent children, she approaches partnered life in a practical rather than romantic state of mind. Her narrative typifies the pragmatic approach of middle-aged women after a breakup:

> INTERVIEWER: Did you have any idea about whom you were looking to meet [on Meetic]?
> PATRICIA: I didn't have a strong idea, but I knew what I didn't want. I wanted someone I could share things with, someone I was attracted to, someone middle class, with a clear situation [regarding his marriage status]. I didn't want to wind up with someone – this is very selfish because I myself have children – but I don't want to end up with five kids every other weekend. I'd have a hard time seeing myself in that situation. And I don't want any conflicts. Because when you're forty, you're bound to come across a man who's separated. That means he has a past, and an ex-wife, and children; you have to deal with all that. (Patricia, 38, registered nurse, two young children)

The Age of Singles 135

One reason why women are more pragmatic after a separation is that they need to address new constraints in reconciling parenthood with couple life. Their first priority is often their children, and future options must be considered in the light of a recomposed family. These constraints are generally greater for women than for men of the same age. Not only do women establish couples and become parents at younger ages than men but, after a divorce or separation, regardless of legal custody issues, mothers are more likely than fathers to assume responsibility for raising their children. In France in 2018, 85% of single-parent households were headed by a woman (Algava et al., 2020).

The situation is different for divorced or separated fathers, who rarely have primary responsibility for children and therefore feel free to start afresh. Unlike mothers, who are objectively and subjectively marked by their parental and conjugal past, men who emerge from a breakup tend to consider themselves rejuvenated. This results in a feeling of almost carefree freedom, which emerges from Bruno's account of discussions with his future partner:

> When we met on Meetic, the first thing she said was that I live far away. That can be a problem. And I said, "Yes, it can be complicated at first, but we'll have to see whether we get along, whether the feeling's right..." I know that the house I'm living in is my own house, I've rebuilt it, but there's nothing keeping me there [...] For love, I could have crossed the ocean. Even though I have two children who are here, who are in Troyes, who are 13 and 15 now. But that won't be an obstacle for me anymore. (Bruno, 44, welder, two teenage children)

After his divorce, Bruno wants to start from scratch and feels free to do so. Bruno turned to a woman 15 years younger and soon made plans to become a parent again: "I'm still young, so why not a new child?" This attitude is in stark contrast to Patricia's and underscores the difference in men's and women's ambitions after separation or divorce. While they share the same desire to form a new couple, men are more likely to want to start a new life, unencumbered by the past.

136   The New Laws of Love

Single again while their offspring live with their former partner, men are ready for a new start and look for women who are young and likely to share their plans for the future. While young men are by and large indifferent to their partner's age, older men typically seek out younger women, especially after a breakup. The evidence from Meetic is striking: men over 40 almost always contact only younger women (Bergström, 2018). This reduces the opportunities of women in their age group. Just as young women's preference for more mature men leads to the disqualification of young men when it comes to forming initial unions, the desire of older, separated men to meet younger women results in fewer opportunities for older, separated women to form a new relationship. This tendency gets stronger with age, as reported by a woman who compared her own experience of online dating ten years ago with a more recent attempt:

> I obviously didn't have as many opportunities as before. The previous time, I could have one, two or three conversations going at the same time. I had more of an impression that I could choose. This time, I was more selective, but the men were also more selective and they didn't select me. There were just fewer people who were interested in me. I don't think it had anything to do with me. I think it was more a question of what the men were looking for. (Michelle, 49, writer, no children)

Michelle has fewer online contacts than when she was in her thirties, and the opportunities to meet people are more limited. As women grow older, they are first marginalized and then excluded from the dating game. Many women over 50 years of age simply abandon online dating, sometimes after several years in which they haven't succeeded in establishing a new relationship as they wished to do. Like younger men left on the sidelines, but at the other end of the age spectrum, these women are also left out.

These contrasting experiences with online dating confirm the existence of gendered ages. Far from being a simple biological variable plotted on a linear scale, age is measured differently for the two sexes. Men "stay young" longer than women: they are considered to take longer to grow up and, consequently, they go through the steps of transitioning into adulthood, forming a couple, and starting a family later than women. Interestingly, they also become "young again" after a breakup. When women are left to take care of the children, men enjoy greater freedom, both objectively and subjectively. While separation rejuvenates men, it leaves women in a completely different situation. Generally considered more mature than the boys when they are young girls, women are judged by men to be too old after a breakup. These gender inequalities in aging make for experiences of singlehood that are radically different for women and for men at different stages in life.

Social class and couple norms

The strong social inequalities observed among single men are less pronounced among single women. In France, it is rare for women to remain single into their middle years, and this holds for all social classes to the same extent: less than 3% of the women aged 40 and older report that they have never had a significant romantic relationship.[8] This has not always been the case. Historically, permanent singlehood was higher among educated women. Turning once more to Milan Bouchet-Valat's study, we learn that, in France, among the generations born before World War II, "a very clear gradient is observed [for women]; the likelihood of forming a union decreases steadily as their educational level increases" (Bouchet-Valat, 2015, p. 679). In the first part of the twentieth century, women with a bachelor's degree or a higher diploma were significantly less likely than less educated women to have experienced a relationship that involved cohabitation.

Words were often harsh for these highly educated women, many of whom remained unmarried. The historian Harry G. Cocks has documented the concerns expressed by British doctors and psychiatrists in the 1920s over the negative effects of modern womanhood. The independence that followed women's entry into the labor force during World War I was thought to place them in mental danger, as they were "susceptible to loneliness and all its attendant emotional difficulties. They were, in the view of one doctor, 'failures in love'" (Cocks, 2009, p. 52).

These stereotypes have not disappeared. Serge Chaumier found them in the French press throughout the 1980s and 1990s, in articles that explained that successful women – superwomen – cannot have it all: "Women who were [considered] prisoners of their social success were said to pay the price through the failure of their love life." He added that these "media warnings were not devoid of a conservative undertone. They reflected male resistance to change" (Chaumier, 2004, p. 15). The caricature of the liberated woman served as a barely disguised reminder of the gender roles. The message addressed to women who asserted themselves socially and economically was that, if they sought a status equivalent to that of their male counterparts, if they invested in education and in a career, they would have to "pay the price" of foregoing marriage and a family.

The idea that successful women are condemned to isolation remains strong, and articles on the topic are numerous. In 2016, the *Times* explained to its readers that young professional and well-educated women are "starved of a boyfriend" and "losing out in the relationship numbers game"; in this it was echoing a report in the French edition of a 2014 issue of the *Elle* magazine, which stated that, "for a woman, success often rhymes with being single."[9] Yet the statistical basis for these claims is weak. In the past the most educated women were indeed more likely to remain single, but the situation has changed in several countries. In France, for instance, over the course of the twentieth century, "among women, the differences [in union formation] between educational groups [grew] progressively narrower, before disappearing altogether" (Bouchet-Valat, 2015, p. 680). In consequence, in female cohorts born from 1950 onwards, no educational group is more likely than another to experience lifelong singlehood. Similar results are found in the United States, where all women, independently of educational attainment, show high rates of couple formation (Manning et al., 2014). In fact female higher education ceased to be a departure from gender norms long ago, and it is now normal for women to be university graduates. At the same time, combining a skilled career and

The Age of Singles   139

personal life has become much easier. For all these reasons, highly educated women no longer constitute a disproportionate share of single women.

In fact, among women, social inequalities do not affect the likelihood of forming a couple, but rather the *consequences of breakups*. This is clear in France, where women of all educational levels are equally likely to experience separation, but poorly educated women take longer to form a new union and are less likely to repartner than highly educated women. As a result, among younger generations, poorly educated women with low skills are more likely to be single at a given point than women with a higher educational level (INSEE, 2015). The same is true when we compare occupational groups: young female professionals and managers today are more likely to live in a couple than young women in manual or sales-related occupations (Buisson and Daguet, 2012).

But one must be careful of painting too bleak a picture of these working-class women who remain single after a separation. Many do not wish to form a new union. My research with Françoise Courtel and Géraldine Vivier into singlehood in France shows that women from working-class backgrounds often have the most positive experience of singlehood. Without downplaying the economic hardships that follow breakups and are particularly acute for women, and especially for single mothers, being unpartnered brings greater autonomy and independence. This, combined with possible disillusionment at the prospect of couple life, explains why working-class women may not necessarily wish to enter into a new union (Bergström et al., 2019).

Conversely, singlehood is least valued in the privileged classes, and especially among women. This is where we find both the highest rate of people living in a couple and the most difficult experiences of life outside a couple. Contrary to the idea that the upper classes have embraced singlehood as a new way of life, this is where the couple norm is strongest (Bergström et al., 2019). So, against all expectations, it is women from working-class backgrounds, often separated and living alone with their children, who most often claim that singlehood is a deliberate choice. If one takes them at their word instead of cynically assuming that their argument

140   The New Laws of Love

is mere *amor fati* [love of one's destiny], they show that relationship norms are class-dependent and not necessarily linked to economic independence.

* * *

Because of the sheer mass of users and because interest and rejection, attention and indifference, success and failure are plentiful and eminently explicit, online dating makes everyone aware of exactly where they stand. This is clear from how people misrepresent their ages: such lies are not just anecdotal, they are deliberate attempts to improve one's objective chances. On dating platforms, women and men experience at first hand the social and gender inequalities associated with singlehood, as well as the norms of gendered ages.

But these are not new exclusions. As they are subject to the same logic as ordinary dating, these platforms tend to favor people who are already privileged and to disfavor people who find themselves at a disadvantage elsewhere as well. Very young men and older women are disproportionately excluded from dating, both online and in other meeting venues. The two groups may be similar in this respect, but their future prospects are different. At an early stage in the life course, young men are still waiting for a date and, for most of them, this wish comes true. Women at the other end of the age spectrum are more in a situation of exclusion (or definitive exclusion), and some will never repartner. While divorce and separations are a shared experience, they hold in store a different future for members of each sex. Online dating brings this to the light.

But, beyond inequalities, digital dating also sheds light on contrasting attitudes toward singlehood. Although the couple norm may be strong, not everyone dreads becoming or remaining single. Whereas the media tend to picture singlehood as a fashionable new lifestyle among young educated urban elites, it turns out that the socially and educationally privileged groups are the ones least content with being single. In the upper classes, to succeed in life means not only maintaining one's social status but also one's couple life. At the other end of the social spectrum, working-class single mothers appear to be those who make the most of being unpartnered and appreciate it most. Indeed, the power of the couple norm varies according to gender, age, and social class – and not always in ways that we might expect.

7

Digital Double Standards

The privatization of dating makes sexual relations more accessible, especially for those whose sexual conduct is often stigmatized or associated with a "bad reputation," first of all women. However, and this is a crucial point, online dating does not radically change the *terms of access* to sex. On the internet, as in society in general, women are expected to demonstrate a degree of sexual reserve, failing which their respectability, and even their physical integrity may suffer harm. This places on women the onus of moderating hetero-sexual interactions: they are expected to censor their own desires so as not to appear to be immediately available, and they should discipline their own behavior, so as not to give in too easily – while men are expected to take the initiative, notably by making the first move.

These traditional courtship rules are surprisingly persistent and are readily observable online. This doesn't mean that behaviors and gender norms haven't changed over time; they certainly have. Young women's sexual life differs from that of their mothers at the same age, let alone from that of their grandmothers; but it also remains different from that of their brothers. Women and men still flirt, date, and engage in sex on different terms. This chapter presents how *female modesty* works as an organizing principle of heterosexual relations. It is all at once a measure of women's respectability, a

Digital Double Standards 143

fundamental component of the dating game, and a female strategy for counteracting sexual violence. Although the norm applies to women, it regulates men's behaviors and attitudes as well.

Far from confirming the view that dating platforms are places of uninhibited, unrestricted, and outspoken sexual desire, a closer examination of them reveals the complex conditions under which heterosexual relationships are initiated.

Female gaze and sexual objects

Women are commonly thought of as a vulnerable public in online dating, and more generally in the so-called hookup culture. Rather than as sexual subjects in their own right, they are often described as victims of male desire – for example when they give in to casual sex in the hope of commitment – or as pawns duped into adopting male sexual attitudes (or new feminist norms) and trying to play the dating game on the same terms as men – which is portrayed as hopeless, self-demeaning, or just sad. Interestingly, this dual perception of female deception and corruption was already a popular theme in the nineteenth-century debate on matrimonial advertisement (Cocks, 2009; Phegley, 2013; Gaillard, 2020). Historians interested in the journalistic reporting on these ads show that female advertisers were depicted either as vulnerable prey to a dangerous male population or as completely depraved. An article from 1862, published by a New York journalist and cited by William Kuby, illustrates just this: "no girl of well-regulated mind, and with a proper feeling of delicacy and self-respect, would think of responding to the public overtures of a man whom she had never seen, and of whom she knew positively nothing" (Kuby, 2018, p. 30).

There are clear similarities between this nineteenth-century debate and its contemporary counterpart, although today's disapproval does not target women's partaking in online dating but rather their engaging in casual sex. Laura Sessions Stepp illustrates most clearly this concern about young women when she rhetorically asks: "when did teenaged girls

144   The New Laws of Love

– everyday girls, not just the 'fast' girls or the 'loose' girls –
start skipping the smooching and go straight to giving head?
How did they come to believe that offering their services
to guys they barely knew 'was no big deal'?" (Sessions
Stepp, 2007, p. 2). The idea that performing oral sex, rather
than being a mere "service," might arouse women and be
something they engage in willingly does not seem to cross
the mind of this author, for whom sex is clearly "a big deal."

My research indicates that women are less of a vulnerable
population than is claimed in public debate, and that they
do not simply endure, or feel obliged to engage in, casual
sex but most commonly appreciate these sexual relations.
I believe it is clear that online dating, by facilitating access
to sex, especially for women, participates in a female sexual
socialization. Whether we morally approve or disapprove of
it, the fact is that these platforms are places where women
increasingly engage in casual sex and increasingly come to
enjoy it. This is part of a broader evolution of increased
female sexual agency. Whereas women have traditionally
been viewed as mere sexual objects – targets of male desire
– online dating partakes in the historical making of women
into sexual subjects.

Analogously, it gives men a hint of what it means to be
a sexual object. Online dating, through its user profiles,
implies self-staging or managing impressions. The reflexivity
and the auto-reification that result from this process are not
new, at least not to women; the sexualization of the female
body makes many women self-conscious and attentive to
how other people look at them. What is new is rather the
fact that this now also applies to men. Laura Mulvey coined
the term "male gaze" in order to describe the process by
which women are conceived of as objects to be looked at, in
contrast with men, who enjoy the privileged position of being
subjects who do the looking:

> In a world ordered by sexual imbalance, pleasure in looking
> has been split between active/male and passive/female.
> The determining male gaze projects its phantasy on to the
> female form which is styled accordingly. In their traditional
> exhibitionist role women are simultaneously looked at and
> displayed, with their appearance coded for strong visual

Digital Double Standards

and erotic impact so that they can be said to connote to-be-looked-at-ness. [...] According to the principles of the ruling ideology, and the psychical structures that back it up, the male figure cannot bear the burden of sexual objectification. (Mulvey, 1975, pp. 11–12)

This now classic text proposes a psychoanalytical perspective on film theory, but has since been widely used to illustrate the mechanisms of female sexual objectification. Online dating and its visual demands have generalized the process described here. Dating profiles are staged to attract attention and to please. In contrast to earlier matchmaking services such as personal ads, this is an area where image and appearances count a lot, and photos are generally "coded for strong visual and erotic impact," to use Mulvey's terms, and connote the objectification she calls "to-be-looked-at-ness." While the status of object looked at is conventionally assigned to women, men now assume a similar role online. This is a new experience, especially for heterosexual men (whereas many gay men have already experienced the male gaze). In posing for photos, they try to look good and sexy, in order to attract the female gaze. Women in turn browse and flick through profiles and *enjoy looking at men*. Online dating does not overthrow the gendered imbalance that makes women much more subject to beauty standards and sexual objectification. However, it does make men familiar with being evaluated and with the self-awareness this involves, and women with being watching subjects.

At the same time as they give rise to new gendered experiences such as the female gaze described here, dating platforms are also an arena where traditional courtship rules are reaffirmed, and even accentuated. No doubt this is where the image of online dating, as conveyed by the press, clashes most strikingly with how many users interact and negotiate their relationships.

The "bastard" and the "slut"

A common idea about online dating is that heterosexual users, especially those looking for "nothing serious," would

The New Laws of Love

be very explicit about their sexual intentions. Yet this is not the case on heterosexual dating platforms, where interactions often are, on the contrary, very prudish. Gay dating apps serve as insightful examples in this respect, as they give an illustration of what "being very explicit" actually means. To be blunt about one's sexual motives is characteristic of much gay "cruising," and all the more so on dating apps (Race, 2015). In his doctoral dissertation on the usage of online dating among bisexual and homosexual men in France, Anthony Fouet presents and discusses several illustrative examples of the type of chat messaging that may precede gay sexual hookups (Fouet, 2019, forthcoming). With his permission, I have translated in the box here a conversation that typifies much gay online cruising and makes it very clear what straight online dating *is not*.

B, 12.09: Hi
A, 12.09: Hey
B, 12.18: How are you?
A, 12.18: Good
A, 12.18: and you?
B, 12.19: cool
B, 12.19: Looking for?
A, 12.20: Fun
B, 12.21: Now?
A, 12.21: Yes
A, 12.21: Got other pictures? :)
B, 12.21: Yes and you?
A, 12.21: [sends a photo of his face]
A, 12.21: [sends a photo of his butt]
A, 12.21: [sends a photo of his erect penis]
B, 12.29: You're top?
A, 12.30: Yes!!

B, 12.30: [sends a photo of his face]
B, 12.30: [sends a photo of his butt]
B, 12.30: [sends another photo of his butt]
A, 12.31: Nice ass
A, 12.31: You suck well?
B, 12.49: Apparently
B, 12.49: In any case, I love to suck
A, 12.49: Cool
A, 12.49: Free now?
B, 12.50: Yes
B, 12.50: Your place?
A, 12.50: [sends geolocation]
A, 12.50: Yes
B, 12.51: Cool. I can come by for a little while [...]
A, 12.51: Ok

A, 12.51: Where do I cum?
B, 12.52: Face
A, 12.53: Ok
B, 12.53: Are you dominant?
A, 12.54: Yes
B, 12.55: If you like I'm very obedient and submissive
B, 12.55: I can be like your slut
A, 12.57: that'll be cool
B, 12.59: Okay so I'm coming over
A, 13.06: You'll be here in 10 minutes right?
B, 13.09: I'll try
B, 13.10: Ok
B, 13.15: Phone battery is out give me your room number
A, 13.16: 316
B, 13.16: Ok
B, 13.16: Coming

Digital Double Standards   *147*

Men dating other men can openly discuss their sexual preferences, be explicit about what they want to perform and what they expect from each other, and sometimes negotiate the sexual script in small details (as in the example above, specifying exactly where on the body the partner is supposed to ejaculate). While the chat above is a quite representative example of many gay sexual hookups, this type of interaction is extremely rare in a heterosexual setting, where preferences, expectations, and desires are most often kept secret and expressed motives are very vague. Sometimes even the sexual or the romantic intention is not very clear, which means that interlocutors are miles away from discussing ejaculation and fellatio.[1] As Corentin points out, heterosexual desires and intentions are stated between the lines.

> What I find paradoxical about Tinder, from a sociological and psychological perspective, is that it's both disinhibiting and at the same time totally hypocritical. Because in many cases you know very well why you're talking to each other, and why you're seeing each other, but it's rarely explicit. In other words, the application is liberating, because of what's implied. But how much is actually said outright? Far less. Let's say there's a girl you're going to ask over to your place in the evening, after you meet on Tinder. [You ask:] "would you like to come over for a glass of red wine?" [She accepts] and you know very well why we're going to see each other. On the other hand, if you ask, "Are you up for sex?," that's not acceptable, even though it's exactly the same message, but it's almost in a different language from the other. So there's both a genuine liberation – and I think it breaks the codes – and at the same time we see the hypocrisy that's all too human. (Corentin, 25, student; mother: communication manager; father: production manager)

As chapter 4 showed, online dating has made it much easier to meet sexual partners, a feature that Corentin describes as "liberating." However, it has not changed the *terms* of heterosexual dating, which continues to follow a script that prohibits direct reference to sex: it can be expressed, as Corentin says, only in "a different language," through allusion and euphemism. What we see in online dating, as in in-person situations, is the difficulty – or even

148   The New Laws of Love

the impossibility – of articulating desire; hetero*sexuality* does not dare speak its name. This modesty is an imperative for both sexes – an aspect that is rarely addressed.

Many studies have examined the way men judge women by their presumed sexual behavior. In their research on hookups, Laura Hamilton and Elizabeth A. Armstrong stressed the persistence of the sexual double standard according to which women who agree to casual sex readily are "sluts" (Hamilton and Armstrong, 2009). Less attention has been paid to the fact that women, too, judge men according to their sexual conduct. Excessively ostentatious sexual behavior leaves men, too, open to being disqualified. This is what Maëlle explains as she describes her difficulty in answering what "type of relationship" she's looking for online – an information elicited by certain platforms. She considers the question "absurd" – for men and women alike – because of the impossibility of truly expressing one's desires:

> Some of the items are hard to fill in. Like, the "type of relationship" question. The idea is that you fill in whatever you want. But if [a man] says, "I want sex," you're only going to get women who are totally unhinged. And if a girl does that, she'll only get creeps and her life will be a living hell for days! Just for saying that all I want is sex. And if [a man] says, "I only want something casual," he comes across as a bastard clearly. (Maëlle, 25, student; mother: secondary school teacher; father: retired senior civil servant)

To explicitly seek out or propose a sexual relationship comes across as deviant behavior for both heterosexual men and women. While women who do so are "sluts," as Maëlle points out later in the interview, men are "bastards." Both figures are negative, but in different ways; the insults are asymmetrical in the same way as gender relations are.

For a woman, to say that she is looking for casual sex is tantamount to displaying excessive sexual appetite and "giving herself" too easily. This does not necessarily disqualify women as sexual partners, on the contrary: if Maëlle claims that a woman's "life will be a living hell" if she states that she is looking for sex, that is because the woman in question could expect a large number of messages from men. On the other hand, this sexual availability demeans women

Digital Double Standards 149

socially. Another study, conducted and co-authored by Paula England, Shafer Fitzgibbons, and Emily Fogarty, shows that men seek partners who agree to have casual sex, but the very fact of engaging in this kind of relationship makes them lose respect for the women involved. The same logic is at work in the distinction made by some men between girls seen as "relationship material" (respectable women) and girls with whom they hook up ("cheap" women) (England et al., 2008). This means that women's social status is conditioned by their sexual modesty, so that women put their respectability on the line when they engage in sexual relationships.

Conversely, a "bastard" is a man who violates women's sexual restraint. Male and female respondents alike define a "bastard" as someone who "disrespects" and "screws" women. The bastard is therefore a man judged not for his own sexuality but for his behavior vis-à-vis women's sexuality; in other words, the disapproval implicit in this label does not attach to the man's sexual availability, but rather to his attitude toward the supposed availability of his partners. Now the reputation of being a "bastard" or a "fuckboy" (another term currently in use) disqualifies the carrier in women's eyes as a possible partner, but does not devalue him socially. On the contrary, being a "bastard" with girls may be considered a badge of honor in male circles and can receive other men's approval (Pascoe, 2011). The social evaluation attached to the qualifier "bastard" is symmetrically opposed to that conveyed by "slut."

So it is still women's sexuality that is at stake. Both the "slut" and the "bastard" violate the norm of female sexual reserve. This norm is based on a sexual double standard according to which women, but not men, are expected to restrain their sexual activity and to confine it to the couple or keep it in the romantic sphere. Within this framework, casual sex is seen as (and meant to remain) a practice that men desire and women endure. This notion, that only men can really enjoy "sex for the sake of sex," underlies much of the online dating discourse. It is tied to the idea that a transient relationship would inevitably harm or disappoint women, who in the end always want more than just sex. While female and male relational expectations are sometimes in conflict (especially at certain ages, as seen in chapter 3), this does

150 The New Laws of Love

not characterize heterosexual relations *in general*. My own research, like that of Elizabeth A. Armstrong, Paula England, and Alison C. K. Fogarty (2012), shows that many women seek and appreciate casual relationships and hook up with men following their own desires, and without looking for commitment. However, the image of female dislike of casual sex is strong, and it turns effectively into a norm. That is, the statement is not only descriptive but translates into a moral standard for women: "normal" women are not supposed to have the same desires as men (Clair, 2012).

For this reason, women often deliberately project a "serious" image online. Whether they are actually looking for a long-term relationship or for something more transient or casual, many female users claim to do online dating "in the name of love." This may take the form of an explicit statement, in their profile, to the effect that they reject casual relationships (e.g. "not looking for sex," or "only serious dating"); or it may take the form of firmly declining men who approach them in too much of a sexual manner. Indeed, female respondents tend to be put off by an approach that is too obviously sexual, as that kind of approach is considered disrespectful. Consequently, overly explicit written messages are often ignored or rejected:

> Some guys just say it outright, without so much as a "Hi there, what's up?"; it's just "Wanna have a good time?" That's really blunt. Obviously, I assume there must be girls who say yes, because otherwise that wouldn't exist, there wouldn't be any matches, but as far as I'm concerned that approach is going nowhere. (Justine, 21, student; mother: IT professional; father: salesman)

At the time of the interview, Justine had recently broken up with her boyfriend and experienced a period of transient relationships to which she referred as her "short-term arrangements." She had met several men via her app and stated in the interview that she was primarily looking to "have fun." At the same time, she clearly refused to be approached explicitly for this purpose. Her way of reasoning, which many other women share, shows that it is the *approach* rather than the *nature* of the relationship that is called into question. The virtuous image that women project online does not mean that they would reject any casual relations, but rather that they refuse to be approached in an explicitly sexual manner. This attitude does not convey hypocrisy, contrary to what some male users assert. The stance serves a definite purpose and conforms to the codes of conduct that regulate heterosexual interactions.

Male initiative and female modesty

Heterosexual dating, whether online or in person, is regulated by *female modesty*, a norm that guides the behavior of both sexes. Women are expected to display modesty, which involves rejecting any explicit advances and, more broadly, exercising restraint in interactions with men. This means, in essence, not making the first move. Online dating has not released women and men from gendered roles and conventional codes of conduct; on the contrary, these are frequently exacerbated online.

Male initiative is a strong tendency, one that structures every step in the dating process. Men often take the lead by looking for potential partners, signaling their interest, sending the first message, conducting the interactions, suggesting the first in-person meeting, and asking for a second date if the first one is successful. This tendency is evident in many countries (Hitsch et al., 2010; Skopek et al., 2011; Bruch and Newman, 2018), and in physical settings, too (England et al., 2008). On the Meetic Group platforms, male users send far more messages than female users, and a large proportion of first contacts are initiated by men (see Figure 7.1). Differences between countries tend to confirm conventional wisdom about women from Northern European (especially Scandinavian) countries being more active in dating than women from Southern European countries. Indeed, female initiative is more common in the Netherlands (16%), the United Kingdom (20%), and Sweden (20%) than in Italy (14%) or France (12%). However, differences are small, and so are the proportions; male initiative remains predominant. Only the German online dating scene stands out as a place where women more commonly make the first move (31%).[2]

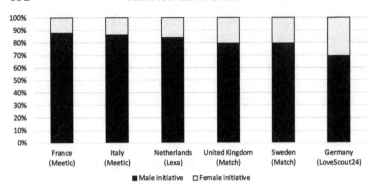

Figure 7.1. Share of female and male users initiating contact on dating platforms in six countries in 2019 (%)

Scope: all initial contacts in 2019.

Source: Meetic Group Databases (Europe, 2019, Meetic Group).

Similar developments are observed on other platforms, for example Tinder, which suggests a general pattern of greater male activity (Tyson et al., 2016).

The male role of initiation is both laborious and unflattering, and some men complain about these gender roles. In an interview, a respondent deplores "how girls operate on Tinder, it's: 'consider yourself lucky you've got a match; now it's up to you to court me, and I'm not going to make the least effort'" (Bertrand, 22). However, female modesty is also a source of pleasure for many men. Another male interviewee says that courtship is "a game of hot and cold in which women are expected to slow things down, while men face the challenge of breaking down the barriers" (Sébastien, 29). Far from being a deterrent, female sexual reserve contributes to building sexual tension in a heteronormative setting and, as such, is part and parcel of heterosexual courtship. Like many men who appreciate this aspect of the dating game, Thomas discusses his discomfort around female initiative and, on the other hand, his excitement about "girls who play hard to get":

> INTERVIEWER: You said that you found it scary if a girl was too direct?
> THOMAS: That's right. I personally can do it, but if someone does it to me, the other way around, well... [...] If the

Digital Double Standards

153

other person comes up and gets right down to the nitty gritty, I feel terribly embarrassed, that's the first thing [laughs]. And then, second, it's too direct [...] I've always liked girls who play hard to get. So I go after girls who aren't easy to get. I'm like a kid [smiles]. I mean, it's a challenge; it's something I can't accept. That's what it boils down to. (Thomas, 21, student; mother: curator; father: business owner)

This "division of labor" or gendered role assignment in heterosexual courtship whereby men are expected to take the lead and women to be unassertive need not be experienced by men as a constraint, and it is often valued highly. Female modesty sets a challenge that enhances a woman's desirability, hence overt signals that she is available may create a sense of discomfort or lack of interest. Female initiative can in fact destabilize the whole courtship ritual:

INTERVIEWER: Was it [the first in-person meeting] the same day?

ERIC: Yeah, it was the same evening. I remember because she's the one who asked to meet. So we'd been talking and all that, a great evening, and then when we were leaving [the bar] she says, "Wanna go fuck?" which totally caught me off-balance. So I was like, "Yes, yes." I tried, and, actually, we couldn't manage. I couldn't get it up because I was too overwhelmed. So we didn't manage. And she was nice; she gave me a second chance so it could happen. (Eric, 37, IT project manager)

This man describes a date unlike any previous experience, in which the woman took the initiative by suggesting that they meet and then have sex. Destabilized by his date's direct approach, Eric was unable to perform. His feelings toward the woman, whom he describes alternatively as a "bombshell" and a "nutcase," are ambivalent to say the least: "She terrified me, she was a little scary." Female initiative, and more generally the absence of reserve, may disrupt the patterns of courtship, destabilize the encounter, and sometimes make it difficult to transition to a sexual situation. Contrary to a common misconception, a woman's overture does not always meet a response. It comes often as

154 The New Laws of Love

a surprise, and is more likely to be met by mistrust and reluctance (Vaughan Curington et al., 2021). Colin here recounts what he considers a very strange experience, in which a woman extended a direct invitation to sexual relations. It was so unusual that he became suspicious and the interaction went no further:

> I had an experience, if you want to hear. It's really crazy. I matched with a photo of an attractive girl, you couldn't see her age, there was no information. [...] I was intrigued because it was mysterious and, after a while, she cut the conversation short; she asked: "What exactly are you looking for on Tinder?" That's when I thought something was strange, and I said, "Nothing serious." She answered, "That's good, me neither; are you free tonight?" and I'm like: "What! What's going on?" I don't know if I would have gone ahead with it, because it would have been too weird. [...] I was deeply shocked by this experience, maybe "shock" is an overstatement, but I was hallucinating. [...] I think it's an urban legend, about the girl who goes "hey there, do you want to have sex, do you want to sleep with me?" The other way around, it's true, there are guys who are sex maniacs, no doubt about that. (Colin, 22, student; parents: salespeople)

Women actively and explicitly looking for sex are an "urban legend" according to Colin. It appears to him unimaginable that such a thing could exist, unlike men who readily seek casual sex – "no doubt about that." What is interesting in the cited excerpt is not whether this particular female initiative was "for real" or not, but the fact that it is so obvious for Colin that it's a "fake." Women, according to him, do not behave like that. They *should not* behave like that. In other words, female initiative deviates from the script that organizes heterosexual courtship, stirring up the roles that women and men are traditionally invited to play. This departure from the conventional scenario not only makes women suspicious; it also makes men unsure about the meaning of the situation and the behavior they should adopt. In both interviews cited here, it is the women's overtly sexual approach that stands in the way of sexual relations. Their behavior, or more generally the manner in which the date unfolds, may leave male partners unwilling or unable to respond. As Eric later added, men have "a hard time managing" these women. Far from being a barrier to sexual relations, some female modesty is often a necessary precondition for a heterosexual relation to come about.

For women, not to conform to the norm of sexual reserve can reduce their control over the subsequent course of events. A woman who signals that she is sexually available takes the risk of being perceived as *unreservedly* and *unconditionally* available; when she does not display the expected sexual modesty, she is considered as having no limits at all. Accordingly, leaving the initiative to men in online dating is a way for women to maintain control over further interactions, as a young female respondent explains:

> I never make the first move. I could, but I don't. I'm just scared. Scared that he's going to want something. I think: If I make the first move, I'm starting something that could lead to something else. So, ultimately, I prefer to let them come to me. (Jennifer, 23, student; mother: cleaner; father: foreman)

Embodying female modesty is more than a matter of self-image or of playing a requisite role in the dating game. It is also a piece of female strategy in creating space in which she could negotiate the nature of interactions as they unfold. Holding back enables women to have their will respected and, most importantly, to assure that men will take "no" for a "no." This strategy is intimately connected to the issue of women's sexuality being linked to their respectability. In a heteronormative setting, women's desires are more likely to be taken into consideration if they conform to what is expected of a "normal" and respectable woman. On the contrary, being considered "easy," "fast," or "loose" comes with the risk of not having one's will respected, precisely because some men lack respect for sexually active women.

Indeed, female sexual reserve is also due to this fear of being violated or forced into doing something one does not want to do. Online dating does not escape the looming shadow of male violence.

Under the threat of sexual violence

A British survey on sexual attitudes and lifestyles in 2012 showed that one woman in ten had experienced sex against her will, by comparison with fewer than one man in seventy (Macdowall et al., 2013). In France, a survey conducted in 2015 found that one in seven women had been the victim of sexual assault; in the overwhelming majority of cases, the aggressor was a man (Hamel et al., 2016). Male violence against women – wives, girlfriends, sisters, daughters, colleagues, friends, or strangers – is a constitutive experience of the condition of being a woman. Women have developed a collective consciousness of their exposure to male violence; the fear of it is not limited to those who have been victims, but goes further beyond. This consciousness is permanently reinforced by the mundane experience of threatening situations such as catcalling, insults, sexist remarks, being groped, or being followed in the street. Even if these events seldom escalate into physical violence, women can never be quite certain and must therefore always be on their guard. This explains why women feel particularly unsafe in public spaces, despite the fact that most sexual assaults occur in private settings and are carried out by people whom the victim knows. The recurrent bad experiences in the street might seem banal, but they "work as real 'calls to order,' a signal to women that they are not in their 'rightful' place" (Condon et al., 2007, p. 104). This situation extends to online dating.

In the same way as walking alone at night is considered risky for women, because they "should not be out alone" (p. 104), meeting unknown men online is seen as potentially dangerous. Male and female users alike believe that the internet is filled with ill-intentioned heterosexual men – referred to as "perverts," "creeps," "sick people," and "psychopaths" – and that women must learn to protect themselves from them. The perceived danger lies precisely in the idea that it could be "just anyone." As a young woman put it, "[o]n Tinder it's like you come across just anyone on the street; he can lie in his profile; it's dangerous" (Agathe, 21). This means that women are encouraged to take precautions. There are many sources of advice for female users,

Digital Double Standards 157

including from the dating platforms themselves, and women often report on the measures they take to stay safe:

> My sexuality might seem frivolous to some, but I'm still very careful about the men with whom I decide to take it to the next level and become intimate with [...] You have to recognize that some people are totally crazy. And there are certain precautions when you meet someone on the internet. Every time, before I meet someone new, I tell one of my friends, "I have a date with someone. If I don't call you in an hour, start to worry." I tell him where I am. I always meet in a public place. It's a precaution. So, there's always someone who knows exactly where I am, and who's waiting for my call: "Okay, I'm safe." (Virginie, 29, social worker)

These specifically female codes of conduct are deeply ingrained in women's socialization. More than being just a matter of common sense, they involve a set of interiorized obligations, with dos and don'ts such as "you must be careful," "you must take precautions," or "there are certain things you must not do." The term "must" picks up the sense of an evident risk of violence; the idea that men are potentially dangerous seems as obvious as the idea that women are vulnerable creatures (Dowling, 2000). The specter of male violence is not challenged, but rather considered natural and recognized as a matter of fact. Women are accordingly expected to protect themselves and to assume the consequences of any infraction; they are held responsible for the risks they take (Lieber, 2008). But the term "must" also expresses the idea of a moral obligation to take precautions. Prudence is a social expectation, regardless of whether or not women are actually afraid or anticipate dangers; they are always expected to be careful in their interactions with men. Women are aware of these expectations, and in interviews they cite the list of "dos and don'ts," although it turns out that they do not always apply them. Being cautious, or even defensive, in interactions with men is to act responsibly.

This amounts to saying that female precaution reflects a framework of sexual morality. This morality also applies to men. In fact, before women apply the female "safety measures," men are expected to do it for them. This appears to be standard practice, especially as the male partner

The New Laws of Love

initiates the meeting. For example, the man will often give his contact information without asking for the woman's: "To keep it safe, I give *my* phone number" (Sébastien, 29). In the same way, men delay the first in-person meeting as a sign of their good intentions: "The idea on the internet is to converse a little, to build up confidence, [to show] that you are not a total nutcase" (Luc, 48).

Men thus assume a protective role, one that is often unrelated to any actual risk. This attitude takes on a ritual form and is part of the courtship scripts. The interactionist sociologist Erving Goffman demonstrates how the ordinary staging of gender relations contributes to the institutionalization of gender differences. He argues that male gallantry is predicated on a representation of women's weakness, from which it follows that "males will have the obligation of stepping in and helping (or protecting) whenever it appears that a female is threatened or taxed in any way" (Goffman, 1977, p. 311). This familiar depiction of female frailty serves to both reinforce and justify gender power relations. In the same way, the precautions taken to protect women on the internet follow a script centered on (and therefore reproducing) female vulnerability. Online dating safety advice – intended for women and justified by the premise that men are dangerous – conveys an ethic of responsibility that, once again, calls on women to show restraint in sexual matters.

To insist on the ritualized nature of the precautions taken by women (and by men toward them) is not to underestimate either women's actual exposure to sexual violence or their fears of this violence. It underscores the fact that violence against women is built into the dating game. Rituals centered on keeping women safe are a constant reminder that violence is always a possible horizon in their interactions with men. It also stresses that women are expected to show reserve in negotiating sexual relations, or else they are considered irresponsible. Regardless of whether or not they personally fear violence, they are compelled to be cautious when engaging in intimate relationships. Thus the threat of violence – both actual and staged violence – contributes to social control over women's sexuality. This factor alone would rule out the hypothesis that heterosexual relations on the internet could become an ordinary, trivial social activity.

Digital Double Standards 159

This will not happen until sexuality ceases to be a sphere in which violence against women is anticipated, feared, and endured.

Terms of consent

Beyond sexual violence, heterosexual online dating is subject to sexual "grey areas," understood as situations characterized by unwanted sex, surprise, insistence or giving in, and leaving one partner – most often the woman – feeling abused, uneasy, or upset about what happened in situations that are not conceived of as sexual aggression, assault, or rape. Feminist writers have criticized the notion of "grey areas" for being a euphemism for sexual violence, and argued that the frontier between consensual sex and non-consensual sex is clear: did she, or did she not, agree to sex? (Jervis, 2008). A British cartoon went viral for humorously comparing sexual consent to accepting a cup of tea: if the woman declines, you obviously do not force her to drink what she does not want to, so why should sex be any different?[3] The message is clear and politically smart, but sexuality is a kind of social interaction very different from having tea, and much more complex.

Theoretically, sexual consent is the active expression of one's will to engage in sexual activity with another person. But such agreements, verbal or physical, like the ones we saw in the gay online cruising chat, are not necessarily a part of the heterosexual script. First, heterosexual courtship is often implicit about sex, as we have just seen, and sexual desire and preferences are largely indicated through nonverbal cues, if at all. This is true not only for initial communications but also for whole sexual interactions, where sex often takes place without discussions among partners about what they like or dislike or what they agree to do or not. One male interviewee, when asked whether he discusses sexual preferences with his partners, stated: "no, you don't bring up the subject like that, no, you often discover that just before sleeping with the person, or even while sleeping with her, you'll understand what she likes, you'll be attentive to what she likes [...] You don't make a detailed plan about the positions you're going to adopt. I find that grotesque" (Louis, 19, student). It is

160 The New Laws of Love

rarer among heterosexual partners than in gay sexual inter-actions to explicitly discuss preferences or the sexual script that is to be acted out together.

Second, since courtship is fundamentally structured by female modesty, the absence of consent, or the ambiguity that surrounds it, is constitutive of the dating game before sexual interactions. Women are not necessarily expected to express desire, but rather to be allusive as to the interest they take in a man. In most situations, the difference between ambiguous flirtation and not being interested in someone (or telling someone off) is obvious from the context and from how lack of interest and disapproval are expressed, but this is not always the case, as this other interviewee explains:

> It's a bit complicated saying to someone "No, I'm not inter-ested in you." Some guys don't get it, either because they're really into you, or they're like "oh, it's a girl doing the girl thing, who tries to play hard to get in order to build up some sexual tension." Except that, in this specific case, that's not it, it's really that I'm not interested in him. But I feel a bit uncom-fortable to tell him that explicitly. (Melissa, 21, student; mother: librarian; father: special needs educator)

These observations show how the norm of female sexual reserve is sometimes considered a matter of interpretation. Women are expected to hold back and often do so, making it sometimes difficult for men to distinguish between staged and actual dismissal. The quotation also underscores a third aspect of heterosexual courtship that widens the sexual grey areas and makes the risk of abuse high: women are often uncomfortable with declining male solicitation and, by the same token, many men have difficulties accepting a rejection. The French sociologist Rébecca Lévy-Guillain, currently writing a PhD thesis on sexual consent, conducted inter-views for the research presented in this book and showed that young female interviewees had trouble expressing their desires in front of a potential partner. Online dating follows quite a formal script that, in theory at least, requires women and men to start by expressing their will to interact (agree to talk), then to take their interaction outside the platform (agree to meet), and then to pursue interactions or not (agree to a second meeting or to sex). Some women show reluctance

Digital Double Standards 161

and unease with online dating precisely because of this need for an explicit consent:

> So, I'm thinking that, if I like the guy, it's cool. But if I don't like the guy, how do you do...? I mean, if you go for dinner, you go for a drink, and afterwards, how do you manage to decline nicely? I got a male friend, whom I talk to all the time, and he's like "go for it," and I'm like, okay, I don't mind trying it out [meeting up in person]. But implicitly, both me and the guy know that we're gonna end up going either to his place or to my place. So what do I do if I don't like him at all? (Lucie, 22, student; mother: housewife; father: farmer)

The question this woman asks herself is, how do I say no? Because she doesn't have an answer to this question, she has not yet dared to take interactions outside the platform. Drawing on her own research, Rébecca Lévy-Guillain shows that many women are not used to speaking their mind, as girls are not brought up to voice their will and desire like boys. This has consequences for many aspects of life, including sexuality. While expressing consent is easier, expressing non-consent is sometimes considered to be difficult. Lévy-Guillain's study reveals that some women do not actually know how to decline in an explicit fashion, or do not dare to express verbally their lack of interest in a man. In order to avoid unwanted situations, they apply alternative strategies, such as coming up with excuses (Lévy-Guillain, 2020). This tactic is also visible among online dating users:

> When that's the case [she does not want to pursue contact], I check my phone on purpose and go like "Oh, I have a friend who just sent me a last-minute invitation for this thing, I had promised to catch up with her, it's been a long time." I invent an excuse. (Deborah, 22, student; mother: pharmacist; father: sales manager)

> I often suggest to meet up at a bar around 9 p.m., I like that because it's after dinner, and it leaves you the time between 9 p.m. and midnight. That way, at midnight, you have a good excuse for leaving and going home [...] It's perfect, that way you can escape at midnight, being like "oh, I gotta catch the last subway train!" (Agathe, 21, student; mother: bank employee; father: unknown)

162 The New Laws of Love

Both these women seek to put an end to the interaction without having to say that they are not interested in the man and that they want to leave it at that. Making up excuses is a way to "escape" the situation, as Agathe says, without having to voice one's will. This female discomfort of speaking one's mind is probably less pronounced in other countries, and dating platforms are undoubtedly used differently depending on context. Jennifer Hicks Lundquist and Celeste Vaughan Curington found that US students appreciated online dating more than campus hookups, precisely because the online conversation "may provide a safe space to communicate one's sexual boundaries, which have implications for building a culture of affirmative consent" (Lundquist and Vaughan Curington, 2019, p. 25).

Other sources tend, however, to show that, in the United States as well, women are less likely than men to decline contact explicitly. The 2019 survey from the Pew Research Center asked respondents how they would express lack of interest if, after a first date, they decided that they didn't want to go out with that person again. Gender differences were the most pronounced among young people (18–29-year-olds), as 60% of the men but only 32% of the women said that they would "contact them and let them know," whereas 57% of the women and 37% of the men declared that they would "not contact them, but would let them know if they contacted you," and 11% of the women but only 2% of the men said they would "not contact them, and would not respond if they contacted you."[4] The results tend to indicate that *exit* rather than *voice* is a female strategy in the United States, too.

This strategy is due not only to women's difficulties in asserting their will, but also to men's difficulties in accepting and respecting a rejection. Once more, interviews with women corroborate the existence of this pattern. While men do not readily admit to being disrespectful or abusive, female interviewees give many examples to that effect:

> I talked to this other guy, but I was not interested in him. I did the big mistake of giving him my phone number and, since he insisted on meeting up, and I said no, because I didn't want to see him, he started insulting me, calling me names. He passed

Digital Double Standards 163

around my phone number, and there were numbers calling me, but I blocked them all. (Agathe, 21, student; mother: bank employee; father: unknown)

Some men do not take no for an answer. The study by the Pew Research Center also confirms this, showing that 60% of female online daters aged between 18 and 29 years had experienced a situation in which someone continued to contact them after they said they were not interested; by contrast, only 27% of the men in the same age group had an equivalent experience.[5] This refusal to accept a dismissal is an illustration of the entitlement that some men feel with regard to female bodies. The thousands of women's testimonies during the #MeToo movement are further proof of this. It is possible that this refusal to accept female rejection, and the violent reactions that it sometimes spurs, are partly explained by the fact that heterosexual men are little used to straightforward rejection: the disproportionate reactions suggest that explicit female turndown is rather rare, and hence is experienced as particularly humiliating – a feeling that is often taken out on the woman. Female modesty and male abuse go hand in hand; both are part of a normative structure that perpetuates gender inequality and sexual violence.

* * *

Heterosexual online dating is fundamentally structured by a double standard. Although it is true that these platforms facilitate access to sex, especially for women, this does not correspond to female sexual emancipation. The very reason why women engage in short-term relations more easily is that the private nature of digital dating makes it possible for a woman to elude normative judgments from her social circle; there are fewer worries about how things might look and what people might think, when the encounter occurs behind closed doors. This means that, while dating platforms temporarily alleviate the risk of sexual stigmatization for women, they also thrive on traditional sexual morality. It is discretion rather than sexual assertion that contributes to making these platforms popular.

Online dating also perpetuates this morality, for at least two reasons. First, privatization is not liberation from moral

164   The New Laws of Love

frameworks. Users bring their values and beliefs when they go online. Just as class dispositions perpetuate social selection on dating platforms (see chapter 5), internalized gender norms prompt female and male users to act differently and to expect different things from each other.

Second, normative expectations are particularly strong on heterosexual dating platforms. By comparison, gay and lesbian platforms provide same-sex relations with an environment sheltered from homophobia and negative reactions. Although discrimination and moral judgments prevail on these platforms as well, the in-group setting fosters a feeling of safety and trust that favors the expression of gay and lesbian desire (Albury and Byron, 2016). This is very different from what we find on heterosexual apps and sites, which are in no way sheltered from sexism. Heterosexuality does not provide a community and heterosexual dating platforms are not a safe space, as women continue to be subject to moral judgments and aggressive behaviors. Conversely, men are evaluated by standards of heteronormative masculinity and are compelled to take on a traditional role of male initiation. In this heterosexual *huis-clos* [secluded space], the normative gaze remains in the eye of the opposite sex. This explains the relatively reserved and cautious use of heterosexual platforms, in particular by comparison with gay apps. Women and men advance carefully, cautious with their own sexual and gendered "normality," and watchful of that of the opposite sex.

Conclusion
Private Matters

It took barely fifteen years for a complete taboo to go mainstream. While matchmaking services have existed for some 150 years, it was not until the advent of digital platforms that their usage became common. The first dating website was launched in the United States in the 1990s, and its heirs gather millions of users around the world today. What was once a marginal, negatively perceived practice is now a familiar feature of singles' life. This makes online dating an exceptional vantage point in the study of social change... and stability. It casts light on the recent transformations of sex and love, but also underscores long-standing patterns that resist change and find themselves reproduced online.

The machinery of matching

Many writings on online dating are critical of this phenomenon. This is especially the case in Europe, where the attacks mounted by journalists and essayists against dating platforms have been particularly acute, targeting as they often do the rationalization and marketization of intimate relationships. The chapters of this book challenge several of the underlying ideas that fuel these critical approaches. In my view, the denunciation of online dating often misses the mark, as it points to underlying mechanisms in partner choice that digital dating merely makes explicit. The critics' attacks draw attention to the self-staging of users, to the comparison and competition between profiles, to the interchangeability, selection, and elimination of potential partners and to the sometimes harsh criteria involved in this process. To be sure, all these aspects are part and parcel of online dating. But are they really new?

Much of the logic at work on dating platforms is not absent from ordinary dating. When individuals go to a party, dressed up and hence self-staged, they may screen the room for potential partners and, on the basis of social and physical criteria, make instant judgments regarding who is interesting (selection) and who is not (rejection). We know from surveys that couples tend to be homogamous in terms of age, class, and race, which means that partner choice is intrinsically selective and discriminating. This is true for relationships that start both online and in person; but in physical settings these selection mechanisms work in a subtle and often tacit way. Choice can be signaled through eye contact and smile, and rejection rarely needs to be spelled out, all it requires is not to make a move. On the internet, on the other hand, the realities and inequalities of dating are exposed to the light of day. Because dating platforms are explicitly and specifically dedicated to romantic and sexual encounters, they reveal the otherwise hidden mechanisms of matching: these become now visible and tangible, primarily to the users themselves. Some are successful, others are not; love is not blind – neither is sexuality.

These are not new truths. Rather they are patterns that dating sites and apps bring to the fore. What these platforms have done was not to set new rules, but to make existing ones very visible. More than anything, online dating renders the terms of heterosexual encounters explicit: on the internet, the machinery of dating is laid bare. This exposure of how dating and matching actually work challenges not so much the realities of sex and love as the imaginaries about them. Online dating works as a magnifying mirror of our intimate relationships; but, as we don't like the picture it reflects, we tend to say that it's the platforms' fault. The market

Conclusion: Private Matters 167

especially, but also algorithms, often serve as scapegoats for the selective and discriminatory nature of dating. We choose to blame the medium.

This focus draws attention away from the real novelty of online dating, which has largely gone unnoticed. Indeed, the emergence of a dating industry has considerable consequences, to which I am turning now.

Private versus public

From a historical perspective, the most radical change introduced by online dating is the disconnection these platforms operate between dating and sociability. At least since the nineteenth century, meeting venues have largely coincided with ordinary social settings in the western world: for the most part, people met partners in their own surroundings. This was and remains true especially for the heterosexual population: the most common way to find a spouse in Germany and in the United States is through family and friends, while work and school come next. Dating platforms rank third in both countries and are on the rise. While these commercial intermediaries have not completely displaced other meeting venues and possibly never will, their unprecedented success raises questions about the changing nature of social life. As the chapters of this book have shown from many different angles, online dating relies primarily on a process of *privatization*.

The word "private" and its opposite, "public," are polysemous. As the social and political theorist Jeff Weintraub (1997) points out, there are at least four ways of understanding this opposition: as a distinction between state administration and market economy (the liberal–economist approach); as a distinction between citizenship and private interests (the republican approach); as a distinction between productive and reproductive spheres (the feminist materialist approach); and as a distinction between collective and personal life (the social historical approach). My perspective adopts this fourth and last approach. Drawing on a definition proposed by the historian Philippe Ariès, I see public and private as two different areas of *sociability*. In this sense, the

168   The New Laws of Love

private sphere is associated with indoor social life and close relationships, whereas the public sphere extends to outdoor environments and larger gatherings, such as "'a public park' or 'public place,'" that is, "a place where people who do not know each other can meet and enjoy each other's company" (Ariès, 1993, p. 9).

According to this definition, "private" (or "privacy") has two different aspects (Weintraub, 1997). One is conveyed by the notion of something's being *personal* as opposed to belonging to the group. In this meaning, activities and objects that are private are restricted to small circles (such as the family), or even to the individual. "Public," on the other hand, designates something that is largely accessible and shared. Hence "public is to private as open is to closed" (Starr, 1988, p. 7). The other aspect of privacy is conveyed by the notion of *secrecy*, as opposed to visibility. In this sense, "private" refers to something that is withdrawn or hidden, in contrast to things that are uncovered or free for all to see. From this angle, private is to public as the opaque is to the transparent (Starr, 1988). Online dating is private in both these senses. As such, it takes part of a broader movement of privatization of social life.

A history of privatized life

A History of Private Life is an imposing five-volume book published throughout the 1980s. This ambitious project set out to capture the transformation of social life in Europe, from ancient Rome to modern times. A variety of authors, carefully documenting various aspects of ordinary life such as work, family, friendship, celebrations, possessions, and aspirations, depict a progressive change in the way of living – a change that amounts to a progressive expansion of the personal realm. The reference point is the end of the Middle Ages. At that time, the individual was largely defined and governed by community, and life was mostly lived in public. This means that many activities, including the most intimate ones, took place in plain sight (see Ariès et al., 1993). The following centuries witnessed progressive but profound changes, as European societies went from

Conclusion: Private Matters   *169*

an almost entirely public to a largely private way of life. Socializing in the streets, in the courtyard, and in the square was progressively replaced by a more sheltered social life, which took place increasingly within the confines of the home. These changes have several explanations, all at once political, economic, religious, and cultural, and were visible for the first time among the privileged classes. The Victorian bourgeoisie of the nineteenth century is emblematic of the emphasis that came to be placed on privacy and domesticity. At the same time, private life became increasingly associated with women, as opposed to public life (both professional and political), which was considered to be in the male domain (Hall, 1985; Digby, 1992). This organization of social life was generalized during the twentieth century, when the home became an important place in all social classes of western societies. Home was now the center of family life, distinct and separated from work (Prost, 1998).

This process of privatization intensified during the second half of the twentieth century. Barry Wellman spent much of his career studying the changing nature of social networks in North America. The postwar period saw a shift in community bonds as local groups of kin and neighbors transmuted into sparsely knit and fragmented personal networks (Wellman, 1999; Rainie and Wellman, 2012). Drawing on long-running research in Toronto, Canada, in the 1970s, Wellman showed that people had loose ties to their neighbors, as social interactions had moved into private homes (Wellman, 1979, 1999).

Recent surveys show a similar trend in the United States that has been growing over time. Between 1974 and 2008, the time spent socializing with neighbors or going to bars decreased, whereas the time spent in social evenings with friends was stable and family time increased (Marsden and Srivastava, 2012).[1] According to Wellman (1999, p. 102), this points to a domestication and privatization of community life: "rather than being accessible to others in public places, people now overcome their isolation by getting together in each other's homes or by the private media of the telephone and electronic mail." Conversely, public spaces have become "residual places to pass through, to shop in, or to loiter in isolation" (p. 83). This pattern is particularly visible in the

170 The New Laws of Love

United States and Canada, where the process of suburbanization has drained public space of social life in a significant way.

This change in sociability is most notable for men and, among them, for working-class men. "Customarily," Wellman noted, "men have gathered in communal, quasipublic networks" associated with work, sports clubs, pubs, or the street, but in the latter part of the twentieth century male friendship progressively retreated into the household and become associated with living as a couple (p. 76). This means that, at the very time when women were gaining access to the public sphere, mostly through participation in the work force, men's socializing moved indoors and narrowed down.

A similar trend has been documented in France by ethnographers who studied working-class culture (Schwartz, 1990; Coquard, 2019). Drawing on extensive fieldwork in the rural and poor regions of eastern France and focusing on male sociability, Benoît Coquard shows that young people's social networks have become geographically extended, but that socially they have narrowed. Whereas previous generations had their social life connected to the town or village and organized around local industries and public institutions such as the village pub, younger generations live and work at great distance from family and friends, and their social life revolves around private events at home. The pub was open to anyone, but private parties are closed environments, so sociability has become much more private. But, even more notably, public space has come to earn a bad reputation. To be a "respectable" young person today, one has to socialize inside, in a private place, with one's acquaintances. To avoid tarnishing their reputation, young people no longer hang out in the streets or at the local bar (Coquard, 2019).

The traditional distinction between a male public sphere and a female private domain is thus fading in the western world, as the privatization of sociability now applies to both genders and to a broad spectrum of society. Only the most precarious populations seem to be excluded from this process: homeless people, but also residents in poor neighborhoods characterized by overcrowded housing (Oliver, 2006). This is not to say that public socializing has entirely vanished.

Conclusion: Private Matters 171

The urban revival of downtown areas in North American cities is evidence to the contrary (Ford, 2003), and many European countries are still known for their vivid street life. Nevertheless, public space is frequented mostly for specific social activities (attending dinner, shopping, going to the movies, visiting a museum, dancing, etc.), which are shared with family and friends, rather than as a place for public gatherings where you meet and mingle with new people. The recent Covid-19 crisis and the subsequent lockdowns that ensued have accentuated this trend in an extreme way, and the consequences on social networks and on socializing may prove lasting.

Online dating is, first of all, a consequence of this privatization of social life. I believe that the trend of narrowing the networks and the premium placed on private socializing at the expense of mixing at public events are reasons for the success of these platforms. The historical rise of private forms of sociability in which participants are already connected one way or the other indeed reduces the chances of meeting new people. As chapter 3 illustrated, this is especially true for middle-aged individuals, who are increasingly single and willing to repartner, but also increasingly removed from scenes where one can socialize with strangers. For these people, the appeal of online dating lies partly in the possibility of bypassing one's immediate social surrounding in order to discover new people.

Yet one should not hastily conclude that online dating produces an opening of social life. On the contrary, online dating brings privatization into the intimate sphere and pushes it even further. By allowing individual access to potential partners away from friends and prying eyes, these platforms make dating more private than ever.

Dating as an island

Online dating is private in the first sense of the word: it is something *personal*. Of course, people may browse profiles in the company of friends, and many users share their online experiences with others; but meeting partners through specialized platforms is different from encounters at school,

172   The New Laws of Love

work, or social events. In those encounters the two partners are linked to each other in some way (through other people, activities, or places) and there may be an audience watching the scene. Dating platforms, on the other hand, rely on a *direct* and *individual* access to partners. Thus the dissemination of these platforms results in a growing distinction between the social and the sexual sphere, between public life and intimate life. Chapter 3 illustrates this particularly well, showing how young people today seek to keep their sexual experiences away from their social networks. There is thus something paradoxical about the use that some platforms make of data from Facebook, allowing them to display connections between users as a sort of recommender system. More often than not, this information is considered a red flag, leading many users to filter these very profiles out. Rather than seeking out partners they are acquainted with, many women and men are reluctant to allow their social life to overlap with their sexual one.

I believe this to be a sign of the growing compartmentalization of social life. Once again, the trend can be read in the light of a broader historical evolution, which points to an increased specialization of activities. For example, in the nineteenth century and before, work and family life were closely associated: the former was often carried out in the home and all family members participated in productive labor. The two spheres would later become progressively separated both in time and space, as work increasingly moved to factories and office buildings, and "working hours" became a notion distinct from "free time" (Prost, 1998). This pattern has expanded. There is today a specific place and time, not only for work and family, but also for leisure, sports, personal time, and socializing with friends. In the historian Antoine Prost's words, we can see both a "differentiation" and a "specialization" of social practices (p. 9). Dating is the latest island – but probably not the last – in this archipelago of activities. Romantic and sexual encounters now have their own place, and are more than before a distinct activity in our calendar.

This distinction between different spheres is not always sharp. Overlappings often occur, but the blurring of boundaries is unequally accepted, depending on the social activities

Conclusion: Private Matters 173

involved. For instance, making friends at work is common, and getting to forge new acquaintances at the local gym is not frowned upon. Meeting one's spouse in one of these ways may be more delicate, but in most countries finding love at work or at the sports club is still considered to be quite romantic. However, having an affair with a colleague or casual sex with one's personal trainer is regarded as more risky; it straddles the lines of ethical behavior. This kind of judgment may be even more pronounced since the advent of online dating. The emergence of platforms specifically dedicated to intimate relationships has fueled the idea that casual sex should be kept out of social networks, especially professional ones, and also away from acquaintances and friends.

In itself, the aim of eliminating sex from ordinary social settings is not new, and online dating is not the only way to achieve it. Holiday resorts, for example, have long served as sites for casual sex, as they, too, are characterized by both insularity and discretion (Bozon and Rault, 2012). Dating apps and websites considerably widen the possibility of accessing, but also *isolating*, sexual relations. Although they are sometimes criticized for catering to short-term relationships, they are nevertheless sought out precisely on account of this feature. Interviews with users suggest a growing opinion that, as sex can now be easily accessed online, it should stay there. This aim to confine sex is illustrative of contemporary sexual morality. While love is a respectable relationship that does not disturb other social interactions, the same cannot be said about non-committal sex, which remains by and large discredited. Undoubtedly there has been both an increase and a broader acceptance of short-term relationships over the past decades. But, in spite of what is often said, the trend does not result in a generalization of sex, but rather in its confinement to a specific place and time. Online dating has made sex more accessible, but it has also assigned casual sex to specific platforms.

Domesticity and discretion

The discreet nature of online dating makes it private also in the second sense I mentioned earlier. Encounters that start

174 The New Laws of Love

online are somewhat hidden from view, unlike encounters in many ordinary meeting venues. This is partly due to the domestic nature of user interactions. With digital platforms, dating has become a domestic indoor activity, as partners can be sought and contacts can be initiated from home. This feature lowers the threshold for young people to enter the dating game and for older people to get back "in the game" after a breakup or widowhood.

More importantly, the discretion stems from the insular nature of online dating. The fact that the participants generally do not know each other and that the chance (or risk) of their meeting again is lower than if they were introduced through friends, family, or colleagues at work means that what happens between the two persons can also stay between them. Users can of course decide to tell friends about their online relationships – and they often do. Once again, my argument is not that online dating is a secret; I rather want to stress the flexibility with which users can decide whether to publicize their sexual relations or not. This is because meeting partners has become a solitary practice – something you may or may not tell your friends the next day rather than something you share with others on location, as when you meet people at a party, at school, or at work.

This discretion makes dating platforms very different from other social media, which rather feed the *publicizing* of private life. Indeed, many of us now widely share our thoughts and opinions on Twitter, publish photos of our homes, children, pets, and vacations on Instagram, and publicly share a great deal of information with various people on Facebook. Dating platforms involve no such public display and are not based on networking. On the contrary, there is no public communication but only private messaging; interactions are strictly interpersonal; only members can access profiles; and connections between people ("matches") are not known to other users. Whereas many social networks make our everyday life more visible to others, operating like display windows of our personal lives, dating platforms have the opposite effect.

This discretion invites exploration. Settings hidden from view are places where one can "allow oneself to express desire and to deviate from the norm" (Schwartz, 1990, p. 31). As many chapters of this book have shown, this easing

Conclusion: Private Matters

of external controls gives more sexual leeway, especially to those whose sexual conduct is subject to moral judgments – primarily women. In this sense, online dating is associated with increased female self-determination and actively partakes in the historical constitution of women as sexual subjects. It does not, however, lead to a weakening of norms. This is an important idea that runs throughout the book. Privatization does not mean deregulation. Online interactions obey codes of conduct, and the social, sexual, and gendered norms that frame ordinary heterosexual dating pervade the digital platforms too, in fact sometimes they are even accentuated there. This is because we are social subjects, and as such we carry internalized dispositions, norms, and habits that we take with us when we go online. The true change is not a weakening of norms but a shift in the modes of control. The absence of prying eyes and the loosening of family control and peer pressure emphasize the internalized control on individual behavior. Online dating makes self-governance the key principle of contemporary sexuality.

Notes

Notes to Chapter 1

1 Todd Krieger, 1995. Love and money. *Wired*, 3, September 3. https://www.wired.com/1995/09/love-and-money.
2 David Gelles, 2011. Inside Match.com. *Financial Times*, July 29. https://www.ft.com/content/f31cae04-b8ca-11e0-8206-00144 feabdc0.
3 Source: Meetic Group Databases (Europe, 2019, Meetic Group).
4 IAC, 2019. *Report of Form 10-K for the fiscal year ended December 31, 2019.* https://ir.iac.com/static-files/329f9793-7b24-4684-86c3-935c0c2a7f98.

Notes to Chapter 2

1 Online Publishers Association, 2004. *Online Paid Content: US Market Spending Report*, May. https://digitalcontentnext.org/wp-content/uploads/2002/08/OPA-paid-content-report-may2004.pdf
2 Laurent Carpentier, 2020. Sites à part pour trouver l'âme sœur. *Le Monde Magazine*, November 20.
3 Caitlin Dewey, 2014. "Back-up husbands," "emotion affairs" and the rise of digital infidelity. *Washington Post*, October 3. https://www.washingtonpost.com/news/the-intersect/wp/2014/10/03/back-up-husbands-emotional-affairs-and-the-rise-of-digital-infidelity.

Notes to pp. 50–63   177

4 Charlotte Edwardes, 2015. Tinder? I'm an addict, says hookup app's co-creator and CEO Sean Rad. *Evening Standard*, November 18. https://www.standard.co.uk/lifestyle/london-life/tinder-im-an-addict-says-hookup-apps-cocreator-and-ceo-sean-rad-a3117181.html.

5 The interview was badly timed as it was published the day before Match Group, the owner of Tinder, became a public company. Visit https://www.sec.gov/Archives/edgar/data/1575189/000110465915079968/a15-16521_16fwp.htm.

6 Google Play Policy Center. https://support.google.com/googleplay/android-developer/answer/9878810?hl=en.

7 App Store Review Guidelines. https://developer.apple.com/app-store/review/guidelines.

8 Lane Moore, 2015. Why do so few lesbians use dating apps? *Cosmopolitan*, November 17. https://www.cosmopolitan.com/sex-love/news/a44476/lesbian-dating-apps-why-they-suck.

9 Lux Alptraum, 2019. A dating app for queer women exists – so why is no one using it? Mic, June 13, 2019. https://www.mic.com/p/a-dating-app-for-queer-women-exists-so-why-is-no-one-using-it-17998951. See also Marissa Lang, 2017. Why lesbian dating apps have failed to connect. *San Fransisco Chronicle*, February 13. https://www.sfchronicle.com/business/article/Why-lesbian-dating-apps-have-failed-to-connect-10924704.php#photo-12324805.

Notes to Chapter 3

1 Douglas Shaw, 2020. Coronavirus: Tinder boss says "dramatic" changes to dating. BBC News, May 20. https://www.bbc.com/news/business-52743454.

2 In 2002, 23% of French households had internet access, by comparison with 46% of German households and 50% of British households. Today all countries have an access rate of 90% or more. Source: Eurostat survey (Europe, 2002–2019, EU).

3 I put "work" and "school" together because these are similar settings, and very much age-dependent. In the United States, 13.5% of American adults met their current spouse through work, and another 13.8% met their spouse through school. In Germany, 12% of the adults between the ages of 25 and 48 have met their current spouse through work, and 10.9% through school.

4 Source: ATP survey, wave 56 (US, 2019, Pew Research Center).

178 Notes to pp. 63–102

5 Source: Pairfam survey, wave 12 (Germany, 2020, DFG).
6 Source: ATP survey, wave 56 (US, 2019, Pew Research Center).
7 Sources: Pairfam survey, waves 10 to 12 (Germany, 2017–20, DFG), ATP survey, wave 56 (US, 2019, Pew Research Center).
8 Source: ATP survey, wave 56 (US, 2019, Pew Research Center).
9 Source: ATP survey, wave 56 (US, 2019, Pew Research Center).
10 Source: Meetic Group Databases (Europe, 2019, Meetic Group).
11 Source: ATP survey, wave 56 (US, 2019, Pew Research Center).
12 Source: Baromètre santé (France, SPF, 2016). Note that this survey asked respondents about partners they met in any online setting (dating platforms, but also other types of sites and apps).
13 Nancy Jo Sales, 2015. Tinder and the dawn of the "dating apocalypse." *Vanity Fair*, August 6. https://www.vanityfair.com/culture/2015/08/tinder-hook-up-culture-end-of-dating.
14 Source: EPIC survey (France, 2013-2014, INED–INSEE).
15 Source: ATP survey, wave 56 (US, 2019, Pew Research Center).
16 Source: Meetic Group Databases (Europe, 2019, Meetic Group).

Notes to Chapter 4

1 Kate Julian, 2018. Why are young people having so little sex? *Atlantic*, December. https://www.theatlantic.com/magazine/archive/2018/12/the-sex-recession/573949.
2 Bradford Wilcox and Samuel Sturgeon, 2018. Too much Netflix, not enough chill: Why young Americans are having less sex. Politico, February 8. https://www.politico.com/magazine/story/2018/02/08/why-young-americans-having-less-sex-216953.
3 Mylène Wascowiski, 2019. Génération no sex: Pourquoi les jeunes ont-ils arrêté de faire l'amour ?, *Cosmopolitain France*, November. https://www.cosmopolitan.fr/generation-no-sex-pourquoi-les-jeunes-ont-ils-arrete-de-faire-l-amour,2033946.asp.
4 Source: EPIC survey (France, 2013–2014, INED–INSEE).
5 Source: EPIC survey (France, 2013–2014, INED–INSEE).
6 Source: ATP survey, wave 56 (US, 2019, Pew Research Center).

Notes to Chapter 5

1 App Luxy. https://apps.apple.com/fr/app/luxy-dating-love-in-france/id873518909.

Notes to pp. 103–63

2 App The League. https://apps.apple.com/us/app/the-league-intelligent-dating/id893653132.
3 App Raya. https://apps.apple.com/us/app/raya/id957215308.
4 App Once. https://getonce.com/en.
5 Source: Meetic Group Databases (Europe, 2019, Meetic Group).

Notes to Chapter 6

1 Source: Meetic Group Databases (Europe, 2019, Meetic Group).
2 Source: EPIC survey (France, 2013–2014, INED–INSEE).
3 Source: ATP survey wave 56 (US, 2019, Pew Research Center).
4 Source: EPIC survey (France, 2013–2014, INED–INSEE).
5 Source: EPIC survey (France, 2013–2014, INED–INSEE).
6 Source: EPIC survey (France, 2013–2014, INED–INSEE).
7 Source: EPIC survey (France, 2013–2014, INED–INSEE).
8 Source: EPIC survey (France, 2013–2014, INED–INSEE).
9 Ellie Austin, 2016. Young, attractive, educated, female – and single. *Times*, May 22, 2016. https://www.thetimes.co.uk/article/the-missing-ingredient-c0lrqcc5p; Daniele Gerkens and Florence Tredez, Amour: Mais où sont passés les hommes?, *Elle*, January 13, 2014. https://www.elle.fr/Love-Sexe/Celibataires/Articles/Amour-mais-ou-sont-passes-les-hommes-2651837.

Notes to Chapter 7

1 In her MA thesis on sugar dating in France, Clara-Marie Nasser (2020) showed that even in a prostitution setting where women negotiate sexual relations in exchange for economic retribution, the exact nature of the sexual act that will take place often remains unspoken.
2 This is also the case on Neu, the other German dating service included in the Meetic Group Databases that I have analyzed.
3 The text was first published, and is still available, on the blog Rockstar Dinosaur Pirate Princess: visit https://rockstardinosaurpirateprincess.wordpress.com/2015/03/02/consent-not-actually-that-complicated. The cartoon can be viewed on http://www.consentiseverything.com.
4 Source: ATP survey, wave 56 (US, 2019, Pew Research Center).
5 Source: ATP survey, wave 56 (US, 2019, Pew Research Center).

Note to Conclusion

1 Peter V. Marsden and Sameer Strivastava's (2012) analysis considered the period from 1972 to 2008. Since then, new waves of the survey have been released. My own analysis indicates that the decline in neighboring and spending time in bars is a continuous trend also between 2008 and 2018. Source: the GSS survey (US, 1972–2018, NORC–University of Chicago–NSF).

Bibliography

Adam, P. 1999. Bonheur dans le ghetto ou bonheur domestique? *Actes de la recherche en sciences sociales*, 128: 56–67.

Albury, K., and Byron, P. 2016. Safe on my phone? Same-sex attracted young people's negotiations of intimacy, visibility, and risk on digital hook-up apps. *Social Media + Society*, 2. https://journals.sagepub.com/doi/full/10.1177/2056305116672887.

Algava, É., Bloch, K., and Vallès, V. 2020. En 2018, 4 millions d'enfants mineurs vivent avec un seul de leurs parents au domicile. *INSEE Première*, 1788. https://www.insee.fr/fr/statistiques/4285341.

Ariès, P. 1993. Introduction. In P. Ariès, G. Duby, and R. Chartier (vol. eds.), *A history of private life*, vol. 3: *Passions of the Renaissance*, translated by A. Goldhammer. Cambridge, MA: Harvard University Press, pp. 1–11.

Ariès, P., Duby, G., and Chartier, R. (vol. eds.). 1993. *A history of private life*, vol. 3: *Passions of the Renaissance*, translated by A. Goldhammer. Cambridge, MA: Harvard University Press.

Armstrong, E. A., England, P., and Fogarty, A. C. 2012. Accounting for women's orgasm and sexual enjoyment in college hookups and relationships. *American Sociological Review*, 77: 435–462.

Armstrong, E. A., Hamilton, L., and England, P. 2010. Is hooking up bad for young women? *Contexts*, 9: 22–27.

Bajos, N., and Bozon, M. 2012. *Sexuality in France: Practices, gender and health*. Oxford: Bardwell Press.

Bajos, N., Rahib, D., and Lydié, N. 2018. *Baromètre santé 2016:*

Genre et sexualité: D'une décennie à l'autre. Saint-Maurice: Santé publique France.

Bakshy, E., Messing, S., and Adamic, L. A. 2015. Exposure to ideologically diverse news and opinion on Facebook. *Science*, 348: 1130–1132.

Bauman, Z. 2013. *Liquid love: On the frailty of human bonds.* Hoboken, NJ: John Wiley & Sons.

Beaujouan, E. 2012. Repartnering in France: The role of gender, age and past fertility. *Advances in Life Course Research*, 17: 69–80.

Bellani, D., Esping-Andersen, G., and Nedoluzhko, L. 2017. Never partnered: A multilevel analysis of lifelong singlehood. *Demographic Research*, 37: 53–100.

Bergström, M. 2011a. Casual dating online: Sexual norms and practices on French heterosexual dating sites. *Journal of Family Research*, 3: 319–336.

Bergström, M. 2011b. La toile des sites de rencontres en France: Topographie d'un nouvel espace social en ligne. *Réseaux*, 2: 225–260.

Bergström, M. 2012. Nouveaux scénarios et pratiques sexuels chez les jeunes utilisateurs de sites de rencontre. *Agora débats/jeunesses*, 1: 107–119.

Bergström, M. 2013. The law of the supermarket? Online dating and representations of love, translated by Cadenza Academic Translations. *Ethnologie française*, 43: 433–442.

Bergström, M. 2016a. (Se) correspondre en ligne: L'homogamie à l'épreuve des sites de rencontres. *Sociétés contemporaines*, 4: 13–40.

Bergström, M. 2016b. Who uses online dating sites in France? Who finds their partner this way? *Population & Societies*, 530: n.p.

Bergström, M. 2018. What is behind the age gap between spouses? The contribution of big data to the study of age differences in couples. *Revue française de sociologie*, 59: 395–422.

Bergström, M. 2019. *Les nouvelles lois de l'amour: Sexualité, couple et rencontres au temps du numérique.* Paris: La Découverte.

Bergström, M., Courtel, F., and Vivier, G. 2019. Uncoupled: Experiences of singlehood in contemporary France, translated by H. Coleman. *Population*, 74: 101–126.

Bernstein, B. 1975. *Langage et classes sociales: Codes socio-linguistiques et contrôle social.* Paris: Éditions de Minuit.

Beuscart, J.-S., Coavoux, S., Maillard, S., and Libbrecht, E. 2019. Music recommendation algorithms and listener autonomy. *Réseaux*, 1: 17–47.

Bogle, K. A. 2008. *Hooking up: Sex, dating, and relationships on campus.* New York: New York University Press.

Bibliography

Bouchet-Valat, M. 2015. Fewer singles among highly educated women: A gender reversal of hypergamy across cohorts in France, translated by Catriona Dutreuilh. *Population*, 70: 665–688.

Bourdieu, P. 1984. *Distinction: A social critique of the judgement of taste*, Cambridge, Harvard University Press.

Bourdieu, P. (ed.). 1990. *Photography: A middle-brow art.* Cambridge: Polity.

Bourdieu, P. 1997. Le champ économique. *Actes de la recherche en sciences sociales*, 119: 48–66.

Bourdieu, P. 2008. *The bachelors' ball: The crisis of peasant society in Béarn.* Chicago, IL: University of Chicago Press.

Bovill, M., and Livingstone, S. 2001. Bedroom culture and the privatization of media use. In S. Livingstone and M. Bovill (eds.), *Children and their changing media environment: A European comparative study*, pp. 85–112. London: Lawrence Erlbaum.

boyd, d. 2008. *Taken out of context: American teen sociality in networked publics.* PhD thesis, University of California, Berkeley.

boyd, d. 2011. White flight in networked publics? How race and class shaped American teen engagement with Myspace and Facebook. In L. Nakamura and P. A. Chow-White (eds.), *Race after the internet*, pp. 203–222. London: Routledge.

boyd, d., and Ellison, N. B. 2007. Social network sites: Definition, history, and scholarship. *Journal of Computer-Mediated Communication*, 13: 210–230.

Bozon, M. 1991a. Apparence physique et choix du conjoint. In L. Roussel and T. Hibert (eds.), *L'Évolution de la nuptialité en France et dans les pays développés.* Paris: INED.

Bozon, M. 1991b. La nouvelle place de la sexualité dans la constitution du couple. *Sciences sociales et santé*, 4: 69–88.

Bozon, M. 1991c. Women and the age gap between spouses: An accepted domination? *Population*, 3: 113–148.

Bozon, M. 2004. La nouvelle normativité des conduites sexuelles ou la difficulté de mettre en cohérence les expériences intimes. In J. Marquet (ed.), *Normes et conduites sexuelles: Approches sociologiques et ouvertures pluridisciplinaires.* Louvain-la-Neuve: Academia Bruylant.

Bozon, M., and Heran, F. 1989. Finding a spouse. A survey of how French couples meet. *Population*, 1: 91–121.

Bozon, M., and Rault, W. 2012. From sexual debut to first union: Where do young people in France meet their first partners?, translated by Catriona Dutreuilh. *Population*, 67: 377–410.

Breen, R., Luijkx, R., Müller, W., and Pollak, R. 2010. Long-term trends in educational inequality in Europe: Class inequalities and gender differences. *European Sociological Review*, 26 : 31–48.

Bibliography

Bretegnier, A., and Ledegen, G. (eds.) 2002. *Sécurité/insécurité linguistique: terrains et approches diversifiés.* Paris: L'Harmattan.

Bruch, E. E., and Newman, M. E. J. 2018. Aspirational pursuit of mates in online dating markets. *Science Advances,* 4, eaap9815.

Brüderl, J., Schmiedeberg, C., Castiglioni, L., Arránz Becker, O., Buhr, P., Fuß, D., Ludwig, V., Schröder, J., and Schumann, N. 2021. The German family panel: Study design and cumulated field report (Waves 1 to 12). https://www.pairfam.de/fileadmin/user_upload/redakteur/publis/Dokumentation/TechnicalPapers/TP01%20Cumulated%20Field%20Report%2C%20pairfam%202021.pdf.

Buisson, G., and Daguet, F. 2012. Qui vit seul dans son logement? Qui vit en couple? *INSEE Première,* 1392. https://www.insee.fr/fr/statistiques/1281430.

Byrne, D., Ervin, C. R., and Lamberth, J. 1970. Continuity between the experimental study of attraction and real-life computer dating. *Journal of Personality and Social Psychology,* 16: 157–165.

Cacioppo, J. T., Cacioppo, S., Gonzaga, G. C., Ogburn, E. L., and Vanderweele, T. J. 2013. Marital satisfaction and break-ups differ across on-line and off-line meeting venues. *Proceedings of the National Academy of Sciences,* 110: 10135–10140.

Chaumier, S. 2004. *L'amour fissionnel: Le nouvel art d'aimer.* Paris: Fayard.

Clair, I. 2008. *Les jeunes et l'amour dans les cités.* Paris: Armand Colin.

Clair, I. 2012. Le pédé, la pute et l'ordre hétérosexuel. *Agora débats/jeunesses,* 1.60: 67–78.

Cocks, H. G. 2009. *Classified: The secret history of the personal column.* London: Random House.

Cocks, H. G. 2013. The cost of marriage and the matrimonial agency in late Victorian Britain. *Social History,* 38: 66–88.

Cocks, H. G. 2015. The pre-history of print and online dating, c. 1690–1990. In A. Degim, J. Johnson, and T. Fu (eds.), *Online courtship: Interpersonal interactions across borders,* pp. 17–28. Amsterdam: Institute of Network Cultures.

Coleman, L. J., and Bahnan, N. 2008. Segmentation practices of e-dating. In C. Romm-Livermore and K. Setzekorn (eds.), *Social networking communities and edating services: Concepts and implications,* pp. 553–265. New York: Information Science Reference.

Condon, S., Lieber, M., and Maillochon, F. 2007. Feeling unsafe in public places: Understanding women's fears. *Revue Française de Sociologie,* 48: 101–128.

Coombs, R. H., and Kenkel, W. F. 1966. Sex differences in dating

Bibliography

aspirations and satisfaction with computer-selected partners. *Journal of Marriage and Family*, 28: 62–66.

Coquard, B. 2019. *Ceux qui restent: Faire sa vie dans les campagnes en déclin*. Paris: La Découverte.

Corbin, A. 1994. Backstage. In M. Perrot (vol. ed.), *A history of private life*, vol. 4: *From the fires of Revolution to the Great War*, translated by A. Goldhammer, pp. 451–668. Cambridge, MA: Harvard University Press.

Coulangeon, P. 2011. *Les métamorphoses de la distinction: Inégalités culturelles dans la France d'aujourd'hui*. Paris: Grasset.

Danielsbacka, M., Tanskanen, A. O., and Billari, F. C. 2019. Who meets online? Personality traits and sociodemographic characteristics associated with online partnering in Germany. *Personality and Individual Differences*, 143: 139–144.

Danielsbacka, M., Tanskanen, A. O., and Billari, F. C. 2020. Meeting online and family-related outcomes: evidence from three German cohorts. *Journal of Family Studies*. https://www.tandfonline.com/doi/full/10.1080/13229400.2020.1835694.

De Graaf, H., Van Den Borne, M., Nikkelen, S., Twisk, D., and Meijer, S. 2017. Main conclusions: Sex under the age of 25. https://seksonderje25e.nl/files/uploads/Sex%20under%20the%20age%2025%20Summary.pdf.

De Graaf, H., Verbeek, M., Van Den Borne, M., and Meijer, S. 2018. Offline and online sexual risk behavior among youth in the Netherlands: Findings from "Sex under the Age of 25." *Frontiers in Public Health*, 6. https://frontiersin.org/articles/10.3389/fpubh.2018.00072/full.

Dean, T. J. 2009. *Unlimited intimacy: Reflections on the subculture of barebacking*. Chicago, IL: University of Chicago Press.

Di Nallo, A. 2019. Gender gap in repartnering: The role of parental status and custodial arrangements. *Journal of Marriage and Family*, 81: 59–78.

Digby, A. 1992. Victorian values and women in public and private. *Proceedings of the British Academy*, 78: 195–215.

Dimaggio, P., and Powell, W. 1983. The iron cage revisited: Institutional isomorphism and collective rationality in organizational fields. *American Sociological Review*, 48: 147–160.

Dowling, C. 2000. *The frailty myth: Women approaching physical equality*. New York: Random House.

Dröge, K., and Voirol, O. 2011. Online dating: The tensions between romantic love and economic rationalization. *Journal of Family Research*, 23: 337–357.

Dumontier, F., and Pan Ké Shon, J.-L. 1999. En 13 ans, moins de temps contraints et plus de loisirs. *INSEE Première*, 675.

Bibliography

Dwyer, Z., Hookway, N., and Robards, B. 2020. Navigating "thin" dating markets: Mid-life repartnering in the era of dating apps and websites. *Journal of Sociology*. https://journals.sagepub.com/doi/abs/10.1177/1440783320948958.

Ellison, N. B., Heino, R., and Gibbs, J. 2006. Managing impressions online: Self-presentation processes in the online dating environment. *Journal of Computer-Mediated Communication*, 11: 415–441.

England, P., Shafer Fitzgibbons, E., and Fogarty, A. C. K. 2008. Hooking up and forming romantic relationships on today's college campuses. In M. Kimmel and A. Aronson (eds.), *The gendered society reader*, pp. 559–572. Oxford: Oxford University Press.

Epstein, P. I. 2010. *Selling love: The commercialization of intimacy in America, 1860s–1900s*. PhD thesis, Rutgers University, New Jersey.

Eurostat. 2020. *Key figures on Europe: Statistics illustrated: 2020 edition*. Luxembourg: Publications Office of the European Union.

Fages, J.-B. 1972. *Miroirs de la société*, vol. 2: *Les petites annonces*. Paris: MAMÉ.

Finer, L. B., and Philbin, J. M. 2014. Trends in ages at key reproductive transitions in the United States, 1951–2010. *Women's Health Issues*, 24: 271–279.

Fjær, E. G., Pedersen, W., and Sandberg, S. 2015. "I'm not one of those girls": Boundary-work and the sexual double standard in a liberal hookup context. *Gender & Society*, 29: 960–981.

Flichy, P. 2001. *Imaginaire d'Internet*. Paris: La Découverte.

Ford, L. R. 2003. *America's new downtowns: Revitalization or reinvention?* Baltimore, MD: Johns Hopkins University Press.

Fornel, M. D. 1989. Une situation interactionnelle négligée: La messagerie télématique. *Réseaux*, 7.38: 31–48.

Forsé, M. 1999. Âges et sociabilité. *Agora débats/jeunesses*, 17: 19–28.

Fouet, A. 2019. "At first it's sex, and then there will be a turn to friendship": Intimate–economic exchanges in the construction of affective and friendly sociability. *Journal des anthropologues*, 156–157: 127–147.

Fouet, A. forthcoming. Les usages sociaux des applications de rencontres homosexuelles géolocalisées à Paris: Scripts, socialisations, spatialisations. PhD thesis, Université Paris Nanterre-La Défense.

Freitas, D. 2013. *The end of sex: How hookup culture is leaving a generation unhappy, sexually unfulfilled, and confused about intimacy*. New York: Basic Books.

Bibliography

Fry, R. 2017. The share of Americans living without a partner has increased, especially among young adults. Pew Research Center, Washington, DC. https://www.pewresearch.org/fact-tank/2017/10/11/the-share-of-americans-living-without-a-partner-has-increased-especially-among-young-adults.

Gagnon, J. H., and Simon, W. 2005. *Sexual conduct: The social sources of human sexuality*, Piscataway, NJ: Transaction Books.

Gaillard, C.-L. 2017. Agence matrimoniale. In L. Faivre D'Arcier (ed.), *Mariages*. Lyon: Éditions Olivétan.

Gaillard, C.-L. 2020. Des mariages à tout prix? Genèse, contestation et régulation du marché de la rencontre (1840–1940). *Revue Française de Socio-Économie*, 2.25: 41–63.

Garden, M. 2008. Les annonces matrimoniales dans la lunette de l'historien. In M. Garden (ed.), *Un historien dans la ville*. Paris: Maison des Sciences de l'Homme.

Giddens, A. 1992. *The transformation of intimacy: Sexuality, love and eroticism in modern societies*. Cambridge: Polity.

Gillmor, S. C. 2007. Stanford, the IBM 650, and the first trials of computer date matching. *IEEE Annals of the History of Computing*, 29: 74–80.

Giraud, C. 2017. *L'amour réaliste: La nouvelle expérience amoureuse des jeunes femmes*. Paris: Armand Colin.

Giuliani, G. 2020. *Gender and age differences in heterosexual couples*. PhD thesis, European University Institute.

Goffman, E. 1977. The arrangement between the sexes. *Theory and Society*, 4: 301–331.

Goffman, E. 1979. *Gender advertisements*. New York: Harper & Row.

Gombault, V. 2013. L'internet de plus en plus prisé, l'internaute de plus en plus mobile. *INSEE Première*, 1452.

González-Val, R., and Marcén, M. 2012. Breaks in the breaks: An analysis of divorce rates in Europe. *International Review of Law and Economics*, 32: 242–255.

Gourarier, M. 2013. The French seduction community: Learning to "be a man." *Ethnologie française*, 43: 425–432.

Gourarier, M. 2017. *Alpha mâle: Séduire les femmes pour s'apprécier entre hommes*. Paris: Seuil.

Hajnal, J. 1953. The marriage boom. *Population Index*, 19: 80–101.

Hall, C. 1985. Private persons versus public someones: class, gender and politics in England, 1780–1850. In T. Lovell (ed.), *British feminist thought: A reader*. Oxford: Blackwell.

Hamel, C., Debauche, A., Brown, E., Lebugle, A., Lejbowicz, T., Mazuy, M., Charruault, A., Cromer, S., and Dupuis, J. 2016.

Rape and sexual assault in France: Initial findings of the VIRAGE survey. *Population & Societies*, 538: n.p.

Hamilton, L., and Armstrong, E. A. 2009. Gendered sexuality in young adulthood: Double binds and flawed options. *Gender & Society*, 23: 589–616.

Hampton, K. N., and Wellman, B. 2018. Lost and saved... again: The moral panic about the loss of community takes hold of social media. *Contemporary Sociology*, 47: 643–651.

Hansen, B. T., Kjær, S. K., Arnheim Dahlström, L., Liaw, K. L., Juul, K. E., Thomsen, L. T., Frederiksen, K., Elfström, K. M., Munk, C., and Nygård, M. 2020. Age at first intercourse, number of partners and sexually transmitted infection prevalence among Danish, Norwegian and Swedish women: Estimates and trends from nationally representative cross-sectional surveys of more than 100 000 women. *Acta Obstetricia et Gynecologica Scandinavica*, 99: 175–185.

Hekma, G., and Giami, A. (eds.). 2014. *Sexual revolutions*. New York: Palgrave.

Hesmondhalgh, D. 2012. *The cultural industries*. Thousand Oaks, CA: SAGE.

Hitsch, G., Hortacsu, A., and Ariely, D. 2010. Matching and sorting in online dating. *American Economic Review*, 100: 130–163.

Huinink, J., Brüderl, J., Nauck, B., Walper, S., Castiglioni, L., and Feldhaus, M. 2011. Panel analysis of intimate relationships and family dynamics (pairfam): Conceptual framework and design. *Journal of Family Research*, 23.1: 77–101.

Illouz, E. 2007. *Cold intimacies: The making of emotional capitalism*. Cambridge: Polity.

Illouz, E. 2012. *Why love hurts: A sociological explanation*. Cambridge: Polity.

Illouz, E. 2019. *The end of love: A sociology of negative relations*. Oxford: Oxford University Press.

INSEE. 2015. *Couples et familles: Édition 2015*. https://www.insee.fr/fr/statistiques/2017528.

Jervis, L. 2008. An old enemy in a new outfit: How date rape became gray rape and why it matters. In J. Friedman and J. Valenti (eds.), *Yes means yes! Visions of female sexual power and a world without rape*. New York: Seal Press.

Jouët, J. 1987. La sociabilité télématique. *Communication et langages*, 72: 78–87.

Jouët, J. 2011. Des usages de la télématique aux *Internet Studies*. In F. Granjon and J. Denouël (eds.), *Communiquer à l'ère numérique: Regards croisés sur la sociologie des usages*. Paris: Presses des Mines.

Bibliography

Joyce, N., and Baker, D. B. 2008. Husbands, rate your wives. *Time Capsule*, 39.5: 18.

Kalifa, D. 2011. L'invention des agences matrimoniales. *L'Histoire*, 365: 76–79.

Kaufmann, J.-C. 2010. *Sex@mour*, Paris: Armand Colin.

Klüsener, S. 2015. Spatial variation in non-marital fertility across Europe in the twentieth and twenty-first centuries: Recent trends, persistence of the past, and potential future pathways. *History of the Family*, 20: 593–628.

Kok, J., and Leinarte, D. 2015. Cohabitation in Europe: A revenge of history? *History of the Family*, 20: 489–514.

Kontula, O. 2015. Sex life challenges: The Finnish case. In J. D. Wright (ed.), *International Encyclopedia of the Social and Behavioral Sciences*, 2nd edn. Oxford: Elsevier.

Kuby, W. 2018. *Conjugal misconduct: Defying marriage law in the twentieth-century United States*, Cambridge: Cambridge University Press.

Lahire, B. 2008. *La raison scolaire: École et pratiques d'écriture, entre savoir et pouvoir*. Rennes: Presses universitaires de Rennes.

Lamont, E. 2020. *The mating game: How gender still shapes how we date*. Oakland: University of California Press.

Lampard, R. 2007. Couples' places of meeting in late 20th century Britain: Class, continuity and change. *European Sociological Review*, 23: 357–371.

Lampard, R. 2020. Meeting online or offline? Patterns and trends for co-resident couples in early 21st-century Britain. *Sociological Research Online*, 25: 589–608.

Lardellier, P. 2015. Liberalism conquering love: Reports and reflections on mass romantic and sexual consumption in the Internet age. In A. Degim, J. Johnson, and T. Fu (eds.), *Online courtship: Interpersonal interactions across borders*, pp. 96–105. Amsterdam: Institute of Network Cultures.

Laumann, E. O., Gagnon, J. H., Michael, R. T., and Michaels, S. 1994. *The social organization of sexuality: Sexual practices in the United States*. Chicago, IL: University of Chicago Press.

Le Wita, B. 1988. *Ni vue ni connue: Approche ethnographique de la culture bourgeoise*. Paris: Éditions Maison des Sciences de l'Homme.

Levinson, S. 2001. *Les "histoires de référence": Cadres socio-temporels et représentations des premières relations sexuelles*. PhD thesis, École des hautes études en sciences sociales.

Lévy-Guillain, R. 2020. L'égalité en tension: En/quête du consentement sexuel chez les étudiant.e.s en France. MA thesis, SciencesPo Paris.

190 Bibliography

Lieber, M. 2008. *Genre, violences et espaces publics: La vulnérabilité des femmes en question*, Paris: Presses de Sciences Po.

Lin, K.-H., and Lundquist, J. 2013. Mate selection in cyberspace: The intersection of race, gender, and education. *American Journal of Sociology*, 119: 183–215.

Litwin, H., and Stoeckel, K. J. 2013. Social networks and subjective wellbeing among older Europeans: Does age make a difference? *Ageing and Society*, 33.7: 1263–1281.

Livingstone, S. 2002. *Young people and new media: Childhood and the changing media environment*. London: Sage.

Lundquist, J. H., and Vaughan Curington, C. 2019. Love me tinder, love me sweet: Reshaping the college hookup culture. *Contexts*, 18: 22–27.

Lyons, H., Manning, W., Giordano, P., and Longmore, M. 2013. Predictors of heterosexual casual sex among young adults. *Archives of Sexual Behavior*, 42: 585–593.

Macdowall, W., Gibson, L. J., Tanton, C., Mercer, C. H., Lewis, R., Clifton, S., Field, N., Datta, J., Mitchell, K. R., and Sonnenberg, P. 2013. Lifetime prevalence, associated factors, and circumstances of non-volitional sex in women and men in Britain: Findings from the third National Survey of Sexual Attitudes and Lifestyles (Natsal-3). *Lancet*, 382: 1845–1855.

Manning, W. D., Brown, S. L., and Payne, K. K. 2014. Two decades of stability and change in age at first union formation. *Journal of Marriage and Family*, 76: 247–260.

Manning, W. D., Longmore, M. A., and Giordano, P. C. 2005. Adolescents' involvement in non-romantic sexual activity. *Social Science Research*, 34: 384–407.

Marchand, M., and Ancelin, C. 1984. *Télématique: Promenade dans les usages*. Paris: La documentation française.

Marsden, P. V. (ed.). 2012. *Social trends in American life: Findings from the general social survey since 1972*. Princeton, NJ: Princeton University Press.

Marsden, P. V., and Srivastava, S. B. 2012. Trends in informal social participation: 1974–2008. In P. B. Marsden (ed.), *Social trends in American life: Findings from the general social survey since 1972*, pp. 240–263. Princeton, NJ: Princeton University Press.

Mazières, A., Trachman, M., Cointet, J.-P., Coulmont, B., and Prieur, C. 2014. Deep tags: Toward a quantitative analysis of online pornography. *Porn Studies*, 1: 80–95.

Mcwilliams, S., and Barrett, A. E. 2014. Online dating in middle and later life: Gendered expectations and experiences. *Journal of Family Issues*, 35: 411–436.

Mercer, C. H., Tanton, C., Prah, P., Erens, B., Sonnenberg, P.,

Bibliography

Clifton, S., Macdowall, W., Lewis, R., Field, N., and Datta, J. 2013. Changes in sexual attitudes and lifestyles in Britain through the life course and over time: Findings from the National Surveys of Sexual Attitudes and Lifestyles (Natsal). *Lancet*, 382: 1781–1794.

Mercklé, P. 2011. *Sociologie des réseaux sociaux*. Paris: La Découverte.

Mignot, J.-F. 2010. L'écart d'âge entre conjoints. *Revue française de sociologie*, 51: 281–320.

Mulvey, L. 1975. Visual pleasure and narrative cinema. *Screen*, 16: 6–18.

Nasser, C.-M. 2020. *Valorisation du capital érotique et rapports de pouvoir dans l'hétérosexualité: Contributions des analyses du Sugar Dating à une sociologie des relations hétérosexuelles intergénérationnelles*. MA thesis, École des hautes études en sciences sociales.

O'Neill, R. 2015. The work of seduction: Intimacy and subjectivity in the London "seduction community." *Sociological Research Online*, 20: 172–185.

Oliver, W. 2006. "The streets": An alternative black male socialization institution. *Journal of Black Studies*, 36: 918–937.

Pakulski, J., and Waters, M. 1996. *The Death of Class*. London: Sage.

Parmentier, M. 2012. *Philosophie des sites de rencontre*. Paris: Ellipses.

Pascoe, C. J. 2011. *Dude, you're a fag: Masculinity and sexuality in high school*. Berkeley: University of California Press.

Pew Research Center. 2012. Smartphone ownership update: September 2012. Pew Research Center, Washington, DC, September 11. https://www.pewresearch.org/internet/2012/09/11/smartphone-ownership-update-september-2012.

Pew Research Center. 2016. 15% of American adults have used online dating sites or mobile dating apps. Report. Pew Research Center, Washington, DC, February 11. https://www.pewresearch.org/internet/2016/02/11/15-percent-of-american-adults-have-used-online-dating-sites-or-mobile-dating-apps.

Pew Research Center. 2018. Teens, social media, and technology 2018. Pew Research Center, Washington, DC, May 31. https://www.pewresearch.org/internet/2018/05/31/teens-social-media-technology-2018.

Pew Research Center. 2019. Millennials stand out for their technology use, but older generations also embrace digital life. Pew Research Center, Washington, DC, September 9. https://www.pewresearch.org/fact-tank/2019/09/09/us-generations-technology-use.

Bibliography

Pew Research Center. 2020a. Dating and relationships in the digital age. Report. Pew Research Center, Washington, DC, May 8. https://www.pewresearch.org/internet/2020/05/08/dating-and-relationships-in-the-digital-age.

Pew Research Center. 2020b. Nearly half of us adults say dating has gotten harder for most people in the last 10 years. Pew Research Center, Washington, DC, August 20. https://www.pewresearch.org/social-trends/2020/08/20/nearly-half-of-u-s-adults-say-dating-has-gotten-harder-for-most-people-in-the-last-10-years.

Pew Research Center. 2020c. The virtues and downsides of online dating. Report. Pew Research Center, Washington, DC, February 6. https://www.pewresearch.org/internet/2020/02/06/the-virtues-and-downsides-of-online-dating.

Phegley, J. 2013. Victorian girls gone wild: Matrimonial advertising and the transformation of courtship in the popular press. *Victorian Review*, 39: 129–146.

Pidoux, J., Kuntz, P., and Gatica-Perez, D. 2021. Declarative variables in online dating: A mixed-method analysis of a mimetic-distinctive mechanism. *Proceedings of the ACM on Human–Computer Interaction*, 5: 1–32.

Pinsky, D. 2019. Doing gender online through flirtation: Digitally mediated romantic interactions among college students. *Reset: Social Science Research on the Internet*, 8. https://journals.openedition.org/reset/1303.

Planck, B. 2014. *Kärlekens språk: Adel, kärlek och äktenskap 1750–1900*. PhD thesis, University of Gothenburg.

Planck, B. 2018. *Vörnuft eller känsla: Adel, kärlek och äktenskap*. Stockholm: Appell Förlag.

Polanyi, K. 1944. *The great transformation: The political and economic origins of our time*. New York: Farrar & Rinehart.

Potârcă, G. 2017. Does the internet affect assortative mating? Evidence from the US and Germany. *Social Science Research*, 61: 278–297.

Potârcă, G. 2020. The demography of swiping right: An overview of couples who met through dating apps in Switzerland. *Plos One*, 15, e0243733.

Prost, A. 1998. Public and private spheres in France. In A. Prost and G. Vincent (vol. eds.), *A history of private life*, vol. 5: *Riddles of identity in modern times*, translated by A. Goldhammer, pp. 1–143. Cambridge, MA: Harvard University Press.

Putnam, R. D. 2000. *Bowling alone: The collapse and revival of American community*. New York: Simon & Schuster.

Race, K. 2015. "Party and Play": Online hook-up devices and the emergence of PNP practices among gay men. *Sexualities*, 18: 253–275.

Bibliography

Rainie, H., and Wellman, B. 2012. *Networked: The new social operating system*. Cambridge, MA: MIT Press.

Rault, W., and Régnier-Loilier, A. 2019. Studying individual and conjugal trajectories in France: Scientific and methodological choices in the EPIC survey. *Population*, 74: 11–40.

Rincé, J.-Y. 1990. *Le Minitel*. Paris: Presses Universitaires de France.

Rivière, C. A., Licoppe, C., and Morel, J. 2015. La drague gay sur l'application mobile Grindr: Déterritorialisation des lieux de rencontres et privatisation des pratiques sexuelles. *Réseaux*, 1: 153–186.

Roseneil, S., Crowhurst, I., Hellesund, T., Santos, A. C., and Stoilova, M. 2020. *The tenacity of the couple-norm: Intimate citizenship regimes in a changing Europe*. London: UCL Press.

Rosenfeld, M. J. 2017. Marriage, choice, and couplehood in the age of the internet. *Sociological Science*, 4: 490–510.

Rosenfeld, M. J., and Thomas, R. J. 2012. Searching for a mate: The rise of the internet as a social intermediary. *American Sociological Review*, 77: 523–547.

Rosenfeld, M. J., Thomas, R. J., and Hausen, S. 2019. Disintermediating your friends: How online dating in the United States displaces other ways of meeting. *Proceedings of the National Academy of Sciences*, 116: 17753–17758.

Rubio, V. 2013. Prostitution masculine sur internet: Le choix du client. *Ethnologie française*, 43: 443–450.

Salecl, R. 2010. *Choice*. London: Profile Books.

Scharlott, B. W., and Christ, W. G. 1995. Overcoming relationship-initiation barriers: The impact of a computer-dating system on sex role, shyness, and appearance inhibitions. *Computers in Human Behavior*, 11: 191–204.

Schiller-Merkens, S., and Balsiger, P. 2019. *The contested moralities of markets*. Bingley: Emerald Group.

Schmitz, A. 2012. Elective Affinities 2.0? Bourdieu's approach to partnership formation in the light of e-dating contact patterns. *RESET: Recherches en sciences sociales sur Internet*, 1. http://www.journal-reset.org/index.php/RESET/article/view/8.

Schmitz, A. 2016. *The structure of digital partner choice: A Bourdieusian perspective*. New York: Springer.

Schmitz, A., Sachse-Thürer, S., Zillmann, D., and Blossfeld, H.-P. 2011. Myths and facts about online mate choice: Contemporary beliefs and empirical findings. *Journal of Family Research*, 23: 358–381.

Schuurmans, J., and Monaghan, L. F. 2015. The Casanova myth: Legend and anxiety in the seduction community. *Sociological Research Online*, 20: 94–107.

194 Bibliography

Schwartz, O. 1990. *Le monde privé des ouvriers: Hommes et femmes du Nord*. Paris: Presses Universitaires de France.

Sessions Stepp, L. 2007. *Unhooked: How young women pursue sex, delay love and lose at both*. New York: Riverhead Books.

Sindberg, R. M., Roberts, A. F., and Mcclain, D. 1972. Mate selection factors in computer matched marriages. *Journal of Marriage and Family*, 34: 611–614.

Singly, F. D. 1984. Les manœuvres de séduction: Une analyse des annonces matrimoniales. *Revue française de sociologie*, 25: 523–559.

Skopek, J., Schulz, F., and Blossfeld, H.-P. 2011. Who contacts whom? Educational homophily in online mate selection. *European Sociological Review*, 27: 180–195.

Smith, A., and Duggan, M. 2013. *Online dating and relationships*. Washington, DS: Pew Research Center.

Sprecher, S., Schwartz, P., Harvey, J., and Hatfield, E. 2008. TheBusinessofLove.com: Relationship initiation at Internet Matchmaking Services. In S. Sprecher, A. Wenzel, and J. Harvey (eds.), *Handbook of relationship initiation*, pp. 249–265. New York: Psychology Press.

Starr, P. 1988. The meaning of privatization. *Yale Law & Policy Review*, 6: 6–41.

Steiner, P., and Trespeuch, M. (eds.). 2014. *Marchés contestés: Quand le marché rencontre la morale*, Toulouse: Presses Universitaires du Mirail.

Strauss, N. 2005. *The game: Penetrating the secret society of pickup artists*. London: Canongate Books.

Tabet, P. 2004. *La grande beffa: Sessualità delle donne e scambio sessuo-economico*. Soveria Mannelli, Calabria: Rubbettino.

Thomas, R. J. 2020. Online exogamy reconsidered: Estimating the internet's effects on racial, educational, religious, political and age assortative mating. *Social Forces*, 98: 1257–1286.

Thomas, W. I. 1923. *The unadjusted girl: With cases and standpoint for behavior analysis*. Boston, MA: Little, Brown.

Toma, C. L., Hancock, J. T., and Ellison, N. B. 2008. Separating fact from fiction: An examination of deceptive self-presentation in online dating profiles. *Personality and Social Psychology Bulletin*, 34: 1023–1036.

Trachman, M. 2013. *Le travail pornographique: Enquête sur la production de fantasmes*, Paris: La Découverte.

Turkle, S. 1995. *Life on the screen: Identity in the age of the internet*. New York: Simon & Schuster.

Turkle, S. 2011. *Alone together: Why we expect more from technology and less from each other*. New York: Basic Books.

Turner, F. 2010. *From counterculture to cyberculture: Stewart

Bibliography

Brand, the whole earth network, and the rise of digital utopianism. Chicago, IL: University of Chicago Press.

Twenge, J. M. 2017. *iGen: Why today's super-connected kids are growing up less rebellious, more tolerant, less happy – and completely unprepared for adulthood – and what that means for the rest of us.* New York: Simon and Schuster.

Twenge, J. M., Sherman, R. A., and Wells, B. E. 2017. Declines in sexual frequency among American adults, 1989–2014. *Archives of sexual behavior*, 46: 2389–2401.

Tyson, G., Perta, V. C., Haddadi, H., and Seto, M. C. 2016. A first look at user activity on Tinder. *2016 IEEE/ACM International Conference on Advances in Social Networks Analysis and Mining (ASONAM)*, 461–466. doi: 10.1109/ASONAM.2016.7752275. https://arxiv.org/pdf/1607.01952.pdf.

Ueda, P., Mercer, C. H., Ghaznavi, C., and Herbenick, D. 2020. Trends in frequency of sexual activity and number of sexual partners among adults aged 18 to 44 years in the US, 2000–2018. *JAMA Network Open*, 3. www.ncbi.nlm.nih.gov/pmc/articles/PMC7293001.

Van de Velde, C. 2011. La fabrique des solitudes. In P. Rosanvallon (ed.), *Refaire société*. Paris: Seuil.

Vaughan Curington, C., Lundquist, J. H., and Lin, K.-H. 2021. *The dating divide: Race and desire in the era of online.* Berkeley: University of California Press.

Velter, A. 2007. Rapport enquête presse gay 2004. Institut de veille sanitaire (INVS), Paris.

Wade, L. 2017. *American hookup: The new culture of sex on campus.* New York: W. W. Norton.

Wang, H., and Wellman, B. 2010. Social connectivity in America: Changes in adult friendship network size from 2002 to 2007. *American Behavioral Scientist*, 53: 1148–1169.

Ward, J. 2017. What are you doing on Tinder? Impression management on a matchmaking mobile app. *Information, Communication & Society*, 20: 1644–1659.

Weintraub, J. 1997. The theory and politics of the public/private distinction. In J. Weintraub and K. Kumar (eds.), *Public and private in thought and practice: Perspectives on a grand dichotomy*, pp. 1–42. Chicago, IL: University of Chicago Press.

Wellman, B. 1979. The community question: The intimate networks of East Yorkers. *American Journal of Sociology*, 84: 1201–1231.

Wellman, B. 1992. Men in networks: Private communities, domestic friendships. In P. M. Nardi (ed.), *Men's friendships*, pp. 74–114. Newbury Park: Sage.

Wellman, B. 1999. From little boxes to loosely-bounded networks:

The privatization and domestication of community. In J. Abu-Lughod (ed.), *Sociology for the twenty-first century: Continuities and cutting edges*, pp. 94–116. Chicago, IL: University of Chicago Press.

Whitley, R., and Zhou, J. 2020. Clueless: An ethnographic study of young men who participate in the seduction community with a focus on their psychosocial well-being and mental health. *Plos One*, 15. https://journals.plos.org/plosone/article?id=10.1371/journal.pone.0229719.

Wilken, R., Burgess, J., and Albury, K. 2019. Dating apps and data markets: A political economy of communication approach. *Computational Culture*, 7. http://computationalculture.net/dating-apps-and-data-markets-a-political-economy-of-communication-approach.

Witt, E. 2016. *Future Sex*. New York: Farrar, Straus and Giroux.

Wu, Z., and Schimmele, C. M. 2005. Repartnering after first union disruption. *Journal of Marriage and Family*, 67: 27–36.

Zelizer, V. A. 2005. *The purchase of intimacy*, Princeton, NJ: Princeton University Press.

Zillmann, D., Schmitz, A., and Blossfeld, H.-P. 2011. Lügner haben kurze Beine: Zum Zusammenhang unwahrer Selbstdarstellung und partnerschaftlicher Chancen im Online-Dating. *Zeitschrift für Familienforschung*, 23: 291–318.